Stephan,

may you find
many warm fuzzies.

Dean V. L.

Life Without Anger

Life Without Anger

Your Guide
to Peaceful Living

DEAN VAN LEUVEN

DeVorss Publications
Camarillo California

Life Without Anger
Copyright © 2003
by Dean Van Leuven

ISBN: 087516-789-6
Library of Congress Control Number: 2003107241
FIRST EDITION, 2003

DeVorss & Company, Publisher
P.O. Box 1389
Camarillo CA 93011-1389
www.devorss.com

Printed in the United States of America

CONTENTS

CONTENTS

CONTENTS

CONTENTS

CONTENTS

Dedication

This book is dedicated to my grandfather William Philpott who learned to be a man without anger, to others who have learned to be without anger in their lives, and to those who learn this way of living, either on their own or with the help of this book.

Acknowledgments

A special acknowledgment to Meri Justis, who unknowingly gave the last little thought needed to motivate me to make the commitment to remove all anger from my life.

Also, I give a special thank you to Dr. Sheldon Cohen. He had the vision to see the power of this work in its early stages. As a professional educator and a wonderful friend, he has been invaluable in helping to develop both the teaching program and the material in this book.

Thank you to Tom Stern, a professional counselor who shared his expertise with me, including some of the exercises I use.

Thank you to the students in my latest Living Without Anger class. The class was based on an early draft of this book. I challenged them to find ways to improve this book and they responded. They were invaluable and appreciated.

To all of you who have offered editing input as I have developed this program, I say thank you. Thank you Diane Morrow, Brian Hayes, Stana Knez, Rev. Sandra Swift, Shea Glenn, Patricia Levine, Kelley Schafer, and Jasmine Williams.

I give special thanks to Abraham Maslow, Wayne Dyer, Gerald Jamplosky and those other great thinkers and writers from whom I have learned many of the lessons necessary to develop this program.

Thank you to my wife Pat, who not only has been helpful in developing and editing this material but has also been patient with the many hours that I have sat behind the computer while writing this book.

Thank you to Suzanne Geraci, who was able to capture so well in her illustrations the message of this book.

Thank you to Stephan Speidel, who was able to capture my personality in the photograph on the back cover.

Thank you to Laura Bellotti, who edited this manuscript and was able to organize my thoughts in a way that makes it much easier for you to understand them.

Especially thank you to DeVorss & Company for recognizing the value of the concepts presented in this book and for having the conviction and the courage to present new ideas.

Finally thank you to God for providing us all with this life experience and for the inspiration to understand and present this message to you.

Preface

Throughout my life I have always had this underlying feeling that I was here in this existence to learn something special. I believe this has something to do with why I chose several diverse careers. I also knew that when I finally learned that something special, whatever it turned out to be, my mission and obligation would be to teach it to others. How to become free of anger is that special learning that I am here to share.

I was born on a farm on the southern Oregon coast. I was actually born on the farm at my grandparents' home. As I was growing up I did well in school and was one of two of my graduating class from high school that went on to college. As a farm boy I grew up strong and was able to pay for my college by playing football. I received a Bachelor's Degree in Psychology from the University of Oregon. I then went to Air Force Flight School and became an aircraft commander and operations officer for the Military Air Transport Division and flew the Pacific Theater from Travis AFB in California. I left the service to work as an aircraft instructor and charter pilot.

I started a small charter airline service, which ultimately failed. I then worked for The Boeing Company as a procedure writer in the aerospace division.

My father became ill and I returned to work with him in the family meatpacking and farming business. After my father died, I attended law school at the University of Oregon and was admitted to the Oregon Bar. For a number of years, I worked in international business law. I specialized in international corporate and tax law, dealing primarily with the movement of money between countries.

I then came back to Oregon and established a small-town law office in the city of Veneta. At that time I became keenly interested in the issue of anger. I found myself dealing with many angry clients in my business. Their anger would upset me as well. I began to think about a better way to live life than with all that anger.

By this time, Abraham Maslow had become known for his work with self-actualization. I became interested in this field and studied the aspects related to personal growth. The concept that we do not have to be angry may seem new to many, but it is a logical extension of this line of thinking.

I came to realize that the benefits of being without anger would be so powerful and life transforming that I wanted to achieve this for myself. The turning point for me was when I made the commitment that I would no longer accept anger in my life. I decided that anger on my part was an unacceptable response. Each time I got angry I would focus on the problem and keep looking for solutions until the anger and the reason for feeling it were gone. Learning how to do this has transformed my life. I feel happy nearly all of the time. Life has become more wonderful for me than I ever thought possible.

I have embarked on a mission of teaching others how to be free of anger. I feel strongly that it is an essential part of what we need to learn so that we can evolve, both personally and as a society.

Although anger is an extremely complex emotion, this book sets forth the lessons I have learned and the tools I have used to become free of it. My hope is that you will find these lessons as transforming as I have. My hope is that some day you and I might meet and talk as two human beings who are free of angst and who care in a loving way about everyone and everything.

Life Without Anger

CHAPTER 1

A Life Without Anger?

As individuals and as a society, we are evolving to an ever-higher level of awareness.

At an earlier stage of human social and mental development, the "fight or flight" response was essential to protect us from the perils that we encountered in everyday life. But as civilization has progressed, we have found it more and more effective to respond intellectually rather than physically to the dangers and problems that we encounter. Emotional responses based on anger have become less effective in solving the situations we face in everyday living. And yet we continue to have such responses—even though scientific studies show that anger and stress are neither good for our health nor for our state of well being. Faced with more and more stress, many of us find ourselves in a seemingly endless cycle of stress, anger and depression.

This book is intended for those who would like to break that cycle, who find that anger is getting in the way of how they want to live their lives. My goal is to show you a better way to deal with the anger arising from our ancient "fight or flight" responses. Not only is there a more effective way to deal with anger in our lives, but there is a way not to even experience anger when facing the situations that previously would have provoked it. As inconceivable as it might sound, it is possible to never experience anger. Regardless of the circumstances you come up against, the individuals you must deal with, the aggravating situations you find yourself in, you can learn to choose a response other than anger.

When you no longer react with anger, what will happen? You will be able to think clearly. You will be able to respond effectively, with the best possible response that your rational mind can create, in each situation that you face. You will no longer feel depressed because you will be living life in a way that makes you feel good about yourself. You will be free to fully enjoy your life. You will face each new day with an eager anticipation of what is to come. All of this will be possible when you move beyond anger.

Joy, happiness, contentment, and peace with the world and those around. These positive states of mind are what await you once you leave anger behind. But getting to such emotional states is not an easy journey. Is it worth it? For those who have made such a journey, the answer is a resounding, OH YES!

You may be reading this book because you have serious problems with anger. Will these methods serve as a miracle cure? No. Will they help considerably? They will if you learn to apply them. Our skill in reducing and controlling anger rests on our awareness of it—what it is, how it works, why we feel it—and our application of the methods for controlling it. If you fully consider and apply these techniques, you can eliminate anger from your life. That is my goal for you!

Would you like to feel more joy in your everyday life? Are you ready to give up the anger and irritation you experience on a daily basis—and to engage in the learning process that this will require? Are you willing to do the work necessary to change your life? The rewards are so sweet. Just consider what your life would be like if you never got angry.

Wouldn't it be wonderful to have your boss come to you with a complaint and to be able to face such criticism without anger? Would you like to react with understanding, rather than anger, when your child ignores the rules you've set for him? Think how much better you would feel if you could accept the way other people do things as being okay, and imagine how it would be to always feel loving towards your mate.

Think of the positive changes that could be made in the world if every member of our society learned to respond without anger. We could raise our children in a safer way so that they would grow to be healthy, happy, and successful adults. Our relationships with others, including our partners and children, would be much more fulfilling. Our careers and businesses would improve. We would not only feel much better about ourselves, we would learn to truly appreciate and get along with others, including those with whom we disagree. If we could all learn to erase anger from our hearts, war, litigation, and crime would all become a thing of the past.

From my own experience, I can tell you that being free of anger is a delightfully liberating feeling. It is worth many times the effort it took me to learn and to change. You, too, have the power to change and to make of your life something joyous. It will take some work to make this transformation, but choosing to read this book is your first step.

I developed this program originally as a way to get rid of my own anger, so I know that it can work. It has for me and for others who have used it. It should be much easier for you, as you will have the benefit of all of the lessons that I had to learn on my own. Many of my students who have used this program have transformed their lives. If you are ready to choose a new way of responding to the difficult, frustrating, stressful circumstances you encounter, a happier, more relaxed and fulfilling life awaits you.

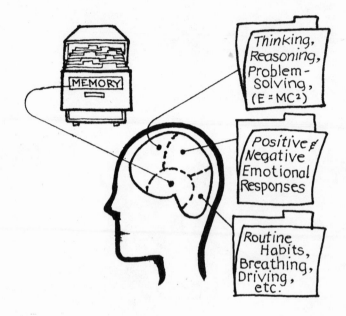

CHAPTER 2

How the Brain Works

In order to understand how the brain works and the relationship between it and the way we act and feel, let us look at the brain in a way that can help us better understand how it functions. We might compare it to a super computer that has emotional and reasoning functions added. The following model of how the brain works will give us a point of reference so that we will better understand how we can make and implement the changes in our belief system that will transform how we view and respond to the world.

At the lower part of the brain is the sub-cortical or "routine habits" area. Routine habits are all the things that we can do without thinking about them, like breathing. It also includes the things for which we have developed habit patterns that are so ingrained that we don't even have to think about them. This can include such simple things as picking up a stick or more complex things like learning to drive a car. Routine behavior is fine until we decide we want to change a response because it is no longer appropriate. Then it can drive us crazy. When we try to break an ingrained habit, it can be very difficult. As an example, after fourteen years, my wife has moved the cereal bowls to the adjacent cupboard from where they have always been. It took me almost six weeks before I was opening the correct cupboard to get a bowl. After three months, I am getting it right most of the time. No wonder that breaking habits like smoking can be so difficult for a long-time smoker.

The limbic system of the brain is located above the "routine habits" area. This is where all of your emotions and feelings are located and where you develop your responses that are controlled by your emotions. This is where you send information that results in any kind of arousal response, which includes both the positive, love-based emotions and the negative or fear-based emotions.

Thinking and reasoning processes are located in the upper portion of the brain, known as the neo-cortex. Here you do your problem solving, such as working out an algebraic equation or determining how you would be able to get to school in order to pick up your daughter after music or basketball practice.

The memory or "file system" is located adjacent to all three of the processing areas. This is where we store all of the information that we have received over our lifetime. In here we have a file on everything. Some are simple self-running files on how to breathe. Some are very complex files, such as how to fly an airplane when one of the engines is not functioning. Every file contains information from our past, and each one has an emotional charge attached to it. Each memory is connected to our feelings, which then determine what we feel—safe, happy, angry, etc.—about a particular thing. For example, I cry at stories of great achievements because of the feelings I have connected in my memory to my father having achieved a great deal in his lifetime.

My father had a tremendous effect on my life. His funeral affected me deeply due to the respect shown for him by his friends and business associates. I cry at funerals now because of that particular memory "file." Before my father's death, I did not cry at funerals.

Most of us respond in a particular emotional way whenever we access a specific file. The messages we receive depend on the emotional charge existing in the accessed file. This is how we create our reality. After awhile we are no longer able to separate the facts we received from the emotional assumptions we made. We merge our interpretation of the event (based on past perceptions) with what really happened and this becomes *our truth*. What we hold as our truth then affects how we feel about new messages that we receive.

All of the information comes into our files via the input sensors, which include our eyes, ears, nose, mouth, and touch. This information is identified and causes a memory file to open. Each of these files contains an emotional charge that is positive, negative, or neutral. That charge is pre-existing in the file and this ignites a particular emotion when the file is activated.

Files with a neutral charge connect to the routine-habits area if we have already developed a response pattern that we can use to deal with the requirements of that particular file. If we don't yet have a response pattern in place, then the file accesses the thinking center. Here we develop a proper response that meets all the needs of this file. If the file has a heavy positive or negative charge, it is then transmitted directly to the feeling center for processing. Here we develop a response based on our emotions. If it is a positive charge, it goes to the love section of our emotion center and we respond out of love. If it is a negative charge, it goes to the fear section of our emotion center (fight/flight/anger) and we respond accordingly. Many files will have a weaker negative or positive charge attached, and we may then access both our thinking and our emotional centers to develop a response.

Sometimes our responses lack a rational perspective relative to the information that we perceive. This is because of the heavy emotional charge we have attached to the particular information we have stored in our files. Psychotherapy is about processing the stuff in our files, sorting out the emotional charges that we have built up in our files. Unfortunately, we are unable to just dump the unwanted stuff in our files and leave no trace of it. We can, however, rearrange the information in a file so that we can interpret what is there in a different way. That is how we recover from mental illness, depression, and stress. It also explains why we can learn to give up the experience of anger.

We create the information that we store in a file by merging our interpretation of the event with what really happened. So our memory is our perception of the event, not just the facts as they happened. This is how we create *our truth*.

Most of us have learned a typical response that we automatically apply when we receive input into one of our files. The message comes in, we open up a file, and what is in the file dictates the response. We can learn to modify how we respond when we receive input into one of our files; however, it's not easy to make such a change. For example, although we may be able to develop a "thinking center-based" response to a particular message, we may still become stressed by that message because the file has left us with an emotional charge that we have not acted on. (Some people refer to this as "stuffing" one's emotions.) We may, on the other hand, respond emotionally, but still be able to modify or control our response based on input from the thinking center. In order to change our response in a way that works well for us, we need to change the way we look at the information that we have in the file (our perception), as well as how we respond to that information.

Throughout the book, we're going to be discussing ways to modify the information in our files so that we can develop different responses to it. For example, we can modify the emotional charges in a particular file. We can also change how we deal with particular charges in processing a file. Or we can place filters in front of files so that we alter the way we perceive the information.

EXERCISE
Reframing Your Thinking

We're all familiar with the old question: Is the glass half full or half empty? When we consider this question, we usually think in terms of only two possible answers. But let's rethink the question for other possibilities. First of all, we have assumed that the question is how much water is in the glass. That is just an assumption on our part. It was never stated as a condition of the question.

In one sense, the glass is always full, unless there is a vacuum in it, or maybe even if there is a vacuum in it. Another way of looking at it is that it is almost empty because of the space between and within the atoms. Remember most of what we think is solid matter is really empty space. If weight is the measure then we need to consider what substance it is because of the different weights. If you think about it for awhile, you will be able to come up with other possibilities.

Our thinking about anger is like that. If we are going to continue to think in the old way, we are stuck with the old answers. But if we expand our thinking, we can find new answers. The common phrase which defines this principle is: "Learn to think outside the box."

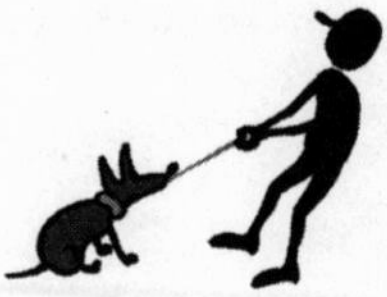

CHAPTER 3

The Real World vs. Our Ideal World

We all function in the same way. However, things appear uniquely to each of us. We each function in a separate reality. Our beliefs come from our experiences, and we make rules for ourselves based on these beliefs. It is difficult to question our belief system because it is self-validating. Information that doesn't match our existing belief system is judged inconsistent with the *truth* and rejected. No one's version of the truth is wrong. It is just different.

A constant source of problems is the conflict between the real world as it actually is and the real world *file* that we have in our brain. We will call what we think of as our real world file, the *ideal world file*, because it represents what we think the world is and not what it actually is. Regardless of how we want the world to be, and how we see it to be, the world is what the world is. The world works the way that it does regardless of our opinion of it. We may see it as working in a certain way or desire that it work in a certain way, but this only changes our perception of it; our perceptions and desires do nothing to actually change the world. We may be able to make some change in the world through our deeds and actions, or by changing the thinking of others, but that is the only way we can actually affect how the world is. We change the real world only by our actions and by how we influence the actions of others. Our thinking, by itself, does nothing to change the world.

As we grow, we are taught certain ideas of how the world is by our society and by those around us – our parents, our teachers, and our friends. We take all of this in and form our own idea of how the world is. We then form expectations of how things should happen in order to fit with our own special idea of how the world is. When things don't happen that way, when reality doesn't match our idea of what we think should happen, we get angry. We need to realize that our idea of how the world is, is only our *ideal world*, as we see it, not the real world at all. If what is happening in the world doesn't conform to your idea of what should be happening, then take it as a clue that your ideal world does not actually match the real world. If you could accept the idea that what is actually happening in the real world is appropriate, then you would have nothing to be angry about.

The ideal world file that we have in our brain just doesn't match the real world. In order to eliminate anger, we need to create a relationship between our ideal world file and the real world itself so that they are not in conflict.

We come into this world and we experience what it has to offer us. However, we influence our experience of this world in several ways:

1. **How we perceive what the world offers.** We react to particular circumstances and events according to our particular sense of right and wrong.

2. **How we accept what the world offers.** Our perceptions about what happens in the world affect how we respond emotionally.

3. **How we respond to what the world offers.** How we respond affects everything that happens after that.

4. **By the choices we make.** The things that happen in our lives come into being as the consequences of our acts.

All of the choices we make affect what the world has to offer. If we choose, for example, to be an accountant, then the world will offer us the experience of being an accountant, and all of the things that go with being an accountant. If you choose to be an angry person, then the world will offer you the experiences of being an angry person.

Why do we respond the way we do? We all have different response patterns. In terms of the anger response, some of us are much better at sending our incoming messages to the brain's thinking center, which helps us to think before we react with anger. Some of us have an ideal world that is much closer to the real world, which prevents anger from rising up. Some of us have developed a way of looking at things (belief system), which is open to new ideas. Some of us have developed a strong acceptance program. Others simply repress anger and stuff it inside. Too many of us act out our anger regardless of the consequences.

Life is not set up so that we can just make a wish and have it granted; our wishes are very often blocked because, quite simply, "life happens." Life offers us trials and tribulations (lessons), and we learn from these lessons what we choose to learn. This learning is what we ultimately get out of life. But if what we learn is simply that life is awful because it constantly blocks our wishes, if we learn that because we're not getting what we want, life is unfair—then our response to life will indeed be an angry one.

If you do not want to be angry at the world and the way it works, then you need to make your world one of preferences. You can say: "This is the way I would like the world to be." And, "I will work to make the world the way I want it to be." And "I enjoy doing this, this is my bliss, this is my way to change the world." On the other hand, you could choose to carry a heavy negative charge on your emotions by thinking, "I must force the situation to be as I think it should be," or, " If the world isn't the way I want it to be, it is wrong." One of the keys to erasing anger from your life is to delete the "musts" in your ideal world. Be ready to accept the real world for what it is. You can work to change the real world when you are in disagreement with it, but accept it as it is for now. Think of it as a world that you have a chance to improve because you have a wonderful vision about how it could and should be. If you choose as your bliss working to make the world a better place, you will be better equipped to succeed if you have a greater understanding of both yourself and the world.

In order to change how we view the world, we must change our basic beliefs about how the world works. When we do this, all sorts of auxiliary or "sub-beliefs" also change.

For example:

> **BASIC BELIEF** – People are good.
> *Sub-belief* – You can trust people.
>
> **BASIC BELIEF** – People are bad.
> *Sub-belief* – You can't trust people.

It is not easy to change our basic beliefs. However, if we want to move beyond anger, if we want to have a joyful life, then we must work to initiate such changes. If we have a belief that results in anger, we will be condemned to hold onto that anger until we change the belief.

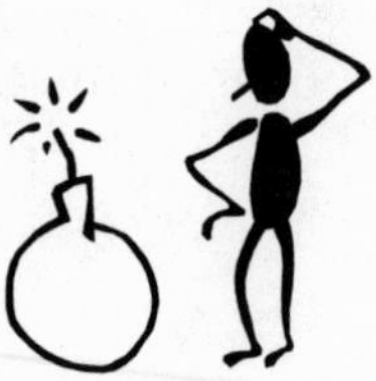

CHAPTER 4

———

What Anger Is

Anger is an emotional arousal to which our reaction is a desire to retaliate or strike back in some manner. It is a negative reaction—a "not feel good" response. I often refer to anger as a "cold prickly" because that describes the way we feel when we are angry. Even if anger is hot and has us "boiling mad," it leaves us with a negative feeling that I call a cold prickly because it's a feel-bad emotion. A positive feeling, or love-based reaction, I call a "warm fuzzy." I learned these terms from two of my grand-daughters. Thank you Kristin and Amanda for bringing these descriptive names to my attention. I love to use them because they give such a clear picture of what we are feeling.

We have positive, love-based emotions, such as joy and happiness. They are warm fuzzys. We have negative, fear-based emotions, such as anger and shame. They are cold pricklys. We feel many different emotional responses, but they all either feel good or feel bad to us. Our primary emotional experience is the need for love. We feel good when we experience it. When we are in fear or anger, we are "out of love" and we feel bad.

When we get angry, what happens to our body? There are changes in muscle tension. We scowl, glare, grind our teeth, clench our fists, flush, perspire, choke, twitch, lose self-control, feel hot or cold. We have chills, shudders, goose bumps, and other physical reactions. There are variations in the way different people feel anger, but we all experience some of these reactions in varying degrees.

Fear is the natural first-level reaction to a threat. Anger is the secondary protective response, and it can motivate us to respond to a perceived threat. Without anger, we are only afraid. Until we learn another way to respond to fear, anger is helpful to us. But anger is a feeling, not an action. It is not the angry act itself, it is what motivates us to act. It is our mental reaction to what we perceive to have happened to us. For example, how another has treated us.

Since anger is an emotion, it is beyond our conscious reasoning. At least it is, at the moment it happens. Emotions are considered to be reflexive or involuntary experiences. The emotion that we feel is something that we do not consciously choose to have or not have at the moment that it is happening.

The Cause of Anger Contains Three Elements:

- Adrenaline

- A stressful event

- A triggering thought

The physical responses associated with anger are the result of adrenaline being released throughout the body. This release is a consequence of a stressful event and then a triggering thought that is associated with the event. The stressful event itself is what we call an arousal and starts our adrenaline flowing. *Whether the arousal is a negative emotion or a positive emotion is determined by our perception of the event.*

Biologically, anger is a stress response of the nervous system, a response to a perceived misdeed, usually by another person. There is blame placed on someone or something, and we feel angry because we believe we have been wronged. We target someone or something outside ourselves as the cause of our anger, because we believe we couldn't feel this way for no reason. There must be someone or something to blame.

Common Forms of Anger:

- Rage
- Irritation
- Impatience
- Intolerance
- Complaining
- Criticism

Anger not only appears in us in many obvious forms, but it also appears in forms which we tend to think of as something else. Some of these forms or emotional states are: disagreeable, disappointed, disconcerted, disgusted, disillusioned, dismal, dismayed, displeased, distant, distracted, distressed, distraught, disturbed, and distrustful.

Stressful events that we perceive as negative are such things as unjust treatment, other people attacking us, having our desires thwarted, and others not doing what we want. In other words, things we don't want to happen are happening.

Triggering Thoughts:

- I demand change.
- I am frustrated.
- They are doing the wrong thing.
- They are trying to hurt me.

Biological research has shown that there is no such thing as pure anger untouched by our culture, our conditioning, and our perception of the event. Anger is a signal that something is wrong and that something must be done to change things. Our idea of what is wrong is created from all of our past experiences and learning.

The physiological symptoms for the love-based emotions are the same as they are for the fear-based emotions. Our mind just interprets them in a different way. The arousal response at both ends of the emotional spectrum comes from adrenaline. Our body re-acts the same to fear and anger as it does to love. If anger shares the same physiological symptoms with love, joy, excitement, and anxiety, then we know that the responses to being aroused are acquired ones that we have developed in our own mind. This means we are responsible for our anger, or any other of our responses. Why? Because if we have learned something, then we can change it. So after an angry outburst, it really isn't suitable to plead, "I couldn't help it," because you could have. Your outburst wasn't caused by the circumstances; it was caused by you. The good news is that since you chose the emotional response in the first place, then you can choose a new and better one to replace it.

Anger/fear is to be used when anger/fear is helpful. In our civilized society, we don't have the need for anger that we had in early times. We don't often face the risk of physical danger that was much more common in the lives of human beings thousands or even hundreds of years ago. Also, we have learned to choose more effective responses by thinking through a problem arising from a particular situation.

Just as we are trained how to respond when something goes wrong on the job or in our profession, we can learn to train ourselves to respond more calmly to situations that would otherwise trigger an angry response. Airplane pilots, firefighters, store clerks, attorneys and others are trained to be problem solvers so that their normal routine is to respond rationally rather than to react emotionally. For those of us who lack such training, anger often results from our feeling of inadequacy in how to deal with the situation. The answer can be as simple as learning how to solve a problem using rational rather than emotional means.

EXERCISE

Become A Problem Solver

1. Write down situations at work where you avoid feeling angry because you have learned to respond as a problem solver.

2. Now write down other situations in your life where you are able to use that same "problem solver" skill.

3. Think about why you are able to respond without anger in the above situations, jotting down your thoughts.

4. Now make a list of other situations in your life when you experience anger, but when you would like to apply those same "problem solver" skills instead.

CHAPTER 5

———

Why We Get Angry

If our anger depends in part on our particular beliefs about the world and how we ought to experience it, then we need to look at where such beliefs come from. Our beliefs about our selves and other people, about the world and how things should be, about how life should be lived, come mainly from our experiences growing up. What we learn from these experiences helps us to develop our unique pattern of responding to life in certain ways.

We learn about anger from our parents, our friends, and our society. We are usually taught that anger is appropriate in certain circumstances. In fact, every book I have ever read on this subject has suggested that anger is normal – that we all express anger at certain times, and that such expression is healthy. This is because we live in an anger-based society. Our society does not have complete trust in the nature of humans, and we are therefore taught that we must protect ourselves from others. We are also taught to expect that things be a certain way. And we are taught to be angry when things are not as we think they should be.

On the other hand, our society often teaches us to repress our upset feelings and to be polite instead. When we do this, we are left with an underlying anger that drains our physical, mental, and spiritual energy. Rather than confronting and solving problems with loved ones or colleagues, we ignore the problems and the feelings. But the anger remains under the surface—and often is expressed in an indirect way.

Sometimes we use anger because it works, and this strengthens our belief that anger is positive. For example, a child will try different techniques—some anger-based and some not—and if anger works, he or she will continue to use it. If temper tantrums produce the sought after result, then a child will make sure to have one when he or she wants to change something that's not going their way. If temper tantrums don't work, the child will realize that and try something else.

In other words, the biases of the mind survive because they work for us. They prevent us from losing confidence in our selves. Our ego seeks only information that agrees with itself. So we need to believe in our own biases in order to have a basis for our very existence. On the other hand, as we're discovering throughout this book, it's possible to have a belief system that is open to examination and change. Such openness comes about when we accept that there's a better way of looking at and responding to our life and our world.

Anger depends on our perception of the situation at hand. We have a curious capacity to believe that life should function just the way we think it should, and we react with anger when our way of doing things is attacked. We can even accept injustice if it is built into our system of how we think life ought to be. Similarly, we accept the roles we play in society if they seem normal to us. We accept giving special privileges to those who govern us because that is what we learn is appropriate. At one time we learned that slavery was acceptable, and that women should not vote. So obviously a society's beliefs change from generation to generation. What is right or wrong is taught to us by our parents, our culture, our government; but it is a subjective standard that we each create slightly differently in our own mind.

HOW OUR EMOTIONS AND BELIEFS INTERPRET AN EVENT

Our emotional response to a particular event is primarily determined by our preconditioning and by our general way of looking at things—our beliefs. But we can also learn to question our beliefs and change our response.

For example, let's say we are driving down the highway. Another car turns in front of us from a side road so that we have to slow down for them. A common response would be to get angry. Why? Because we make the assumption that we have the right-of-way and that the other driver has unfairly taken it from us in a way that has inconvenienced us and inhibited our progress. We do not even consider that, because it's a busy street, the other driver may have to wait another five minutes if he doesn't rush in and slow us down by a couple of seconds.

In the same circumstance, if we choose to react without anger, we might remember having been in the other driver's shoes, waiting at the same intersection, and we may understand why he has acted as he has. In fact, we may even have empathy for his being so rushed and be happy to extend him the courtesy of turning in front of us. As we've said earlier, anger is a choice based on our beliefs. If it is a choice we make, then *not* feeling anger is also an available choice.

We can feel neutral about something. We can feel positive about something. We can feel negative about something. It is our conditioning and the choices that we've made in life so far that set the pattern for how we respond now.

We have many anger-inducing beliefs that hinder our progress in life. Such beliefs are the ones that create negative feelings. They make us angry and depressed and don't help us to deal with life as it really is.

Anger-Inducing Beliefs

- Things should be the way I want them to be.

- It is okay to get angry.

- A parent should be harsh.

- Other people are not trustworthy.

- People should be punished for their mistakes.

- Other people are inconsiderate.

- People take no notice of me unless I get angry with them.

- People are generally selfish and self centered.

- People are constantly trying to put me down.

The problem is that if we see these beliefs as the appropriate way of dealing with things, then we think of our anger as appropriate. Whether we like our anger or not, we think that we must have it because we believe that it helps us to do what we are supposed to do.

Our anger results from our appraisal of a particular situation, which in turn depends on the beliefs we hold, the thought processes we use, the attitudes we practice, and the ways we look at things.

Thought Processes that Commonly Lead to Anger

- *Selective Perception* – We only perceive what we want to (expect to) perceive.

- *Making Unverified Assumptions* – We believe what we think the person meant, without verifying whether that is what they actually meant.

- *Dramatizing* – We dramatize events in our own mind, and we look for the worst possible interpretation.

- *Defiance* – We take an aggressively noncompliant position.

- *Over-Generalizing* – We read more into things than what was meant.

Specific Attitudes that Lead to Anger

- Demanding
- Blaming
- Controlling
- Being intolerant

We upset *ourselves* by making demands instead of having preferences about how things must be. Once we think things must be a certain way, we tend to use anger-inducing thoughts to increase our anger. Our ego likes to make the situation appear worse than it really is because this justifies our anger.

Remember that it is not the event itself that makes us feel angry; rather, it is the anger-inducing thoughts that go through our minds when the event happens. This explains why, under the same circumstances, some people become angered and others do not. It also explains why it is possible to learn to not experience anger.

We look at things the way we do because of the basic beliefs we have developed. These beliefs affect our thoughts and responses, our decisions and behavior.

IS ANGER HELPFUL?

From now on I'd like you to think about anger in terms of it being helpful or unhelpful, as opposed to good or bad, right or wrong. Once you determine that anger is not helpful to you, you can make the decision to choose another way to react. And once you begin to do this, you'll be establishing a habit pattern. We develop habit patterns for most things we do in life, and they are difficult to break. We break one by putting a new habit pattern in its place. And we do this by practicing the new response over and over, until it becomes the new habit.

We are all born with a strong tendency to be creative and constructive and to solve problems that naturally arise in our daily lives. We also have a destructive nature that results in thwarting our progress or undoing the progress we've made. We have the ability to choose either a constructive or destructive way to respond to potentially anger-inducing situations in our lives. It is a matter of training ourselves to respond in the way we want to respond. Which way will you choose?

If we're aware of the beliefs and thought processes that feed our anger, and if we know why we tend to get angry, then we can change our response to those situations when our anger is likely to flare up. We can reprogram ourselves to behave in a different way. Choosing an alternative to anger is within your power. It just takes knowledge, planning, understanding, and persistence.

CHAPTER 6

———

The Things That Make Us Angry

It is important to have a good idea of what causes our anger. If we know the causes, then we can learn either to remove them or to change the way we respond to them.

Most of our anger is caused because the real world does not live up to our expectations or our dreams. We keep insisting the world be a certain way. When it isn't, we get angry. For example, you are in a nice restaurant having dinner and the small children who are part of the family at the next table are being loud and disruptive, and this upsets you. You have an ideal view of how those children should act. You keep demanding that children act that way even though you have no power to control them. And you get angry when they don't do it your way.

We get angry when others in our culture—or outside of it—don't follow the cultural rules. A major role of anger in our culture is its policing function. For example, you expect people to park between the lines in the parking lot at the supermarket. Our society demands this behavior because if people don't follow these rules there will be fewer parking spaces available for other people. When someone doesn't follow the rules and takes up two parking spaces by parking over a line, others often react by getting angry and shouting at them to park properly.

Although every culture's rules are subjective, and different segments of our society may have conflicting rules, anger is employed against those who go against the rules, in order to coerce them into conforming. And because many of us refuse to accept cultural differences as natural and desirable, national governments often use the anger resulting from such differences to justify war.

Sometimes we get angry because expressing anger is an acceptable attribute in our family of origin. Of course one's family has a huge effect on how one deals with conflict. In some families, fighting is seen as bad. In others, you don't even count unless you can stand up and fight for yourself. We not only learn our emotional style from our family, we also acquire the unique set of values our family holds. How our anger gets triggered—and how we express it—are closely tied to the lessons we learned as we were growing up.

We develop a belief system and then get angry when things don't go according to our beliefs. As we explored in the last chapter, our ingrained beliefs lead to disappointment, frustration and anger.

We get angry because we are controlled by our moods. Our moods can have a powerful effect on how we respond. Moods act as filters through which incoming information goes before it gets to our files. When our mood is negative, it increases the negative charge on a file, and when it is positive, it decreases a negative charge on a file. If we are feeling happy, we don't anger as easily.

15 Common Things that Make People Angry

1. Someone or something prevents us from reaching a goal.

2. We say yes when we mean no.

3. Someone attacks us, either verbally or physically.

4. We're unable to relieve our stress so it gets expressed as anger.

5. We feel that we have been treated unfairly.

6. We expect ourselves to be perfect—and we're not.

7. We expect things to go a certain way—and they don't.

8. We expect others to be perfect—and they're not.

9. We want to be right—and someone challenges or disagrees with us.

10. We expect things of others that they're unable to fulfill.

11. We take things personally.

12. We make promises that are difficult to keep.

13. Something doesn't work right, and we feel helpless to correct or fix it.

14. We don't like the way other people do things

15. People don't do what we expect them to do.

This list could go on and on.

"Other people" are a major cause of our anger. When we don't trust others, we think, "I am going to get them before they get me," and we view everything they do with mistrust—which often leads to anger. When we respond angrily due to mistrust, it's as if our brain is out to lunch. We just input information into our "mistrust" file, and we automatically respond from our emotions because we have programmed ourselves in that way. We don't view the behavior of other people as a new problem to solve. Instead, we deal with the situation as one that we already have the answer to. In other words, we deal with the "un-trusted" person as we have already dealt with many other un-trusted people.

Anger Appears when Other People:

- Don't listen to us

- Put us down

- Don't appreciate us

- Tell us what to do

- Intrude on our privacy

- Manipulate us

People don't normally feel angry with others who are of no consequence to them, since indifference is the opposite of emotion. We have to care about something or someone to be angry, but we don't have to be indifferent about something not to be angry.

Hurtful Feelings that can Lead to Anger:

- We are losing our job

- We are losing control

- We are being laughed at

- We are being called incompetent

- We are being called a loser

- We are being ignored

We are not seeking a life without feeling. We are seeking a life without hurtful feelings. And we can do that by eliminating our anger and changing our emotion to love.

▲

EXERCISE

What Makes You Angry?

In order to help you understand your anger better, make a list of all of the things you can think of that make you really angry. Make another list of all of the things that irritate you. Make a third list of your pet peeves.

After each item on the three lists, write down the beliefs and attitudes that might be contributing to your anger. Are you satisfied with how your anger is induced—or do you want to change your response? You can use this list as a basis for establishing a program to eliminate anger from your life.

▼

CHAPTER 7

What Anger Does To Us

Feeling the emotion associated with anger is our first awareness of its presence. But beneath our anger lies a primary emotional pain, such as pride, shame, hurt, frustration, sadness, terror, worry, or fear. Anger is just the way we have chosen to respond to something that has come to our attention that has a negative charge associated with it.

When we get angry, we experience a host of physical changes in our body. There are variations from person to person, but we each experience some of the following responses. Our muscles tense up; we scowl, glare, grind our teeth, clinch our fists, change body position, flush or pale, get goose bumps; we experience numbness, choking, chills, shudders; we perspire, lose self-control, or get hot or cold prickly sensations (thus cold pricklys). We may not all respond in just the same way, but we all experience at least some of these physical manifestations of anger.

Anger interferes with efficient thinking, problem solving, planning, and success. When we are angry, our bodies get hot, our muscles tense, our hearts pound, and our thoughts race out of control. When we're in the midst of such physical reactions, we need to stop and pay attention to what has triggered the angry reaction and why it has done so. Until we are able to relax and think clearly again, we will not be able to act effectively or communicate clearly. Instead, we'll be in danger of choosing angry responses that our reflective reasoning would tell us are ineffective or inappropriate.

Anger can actually get to the point where it makes us physically and/or mentally ill. It causes marital instability, conflict, and divorce. It may limit our educational achievement and occupational success. It makes us poor parents. It stands in the way of intimacy. It can cost us lots of money and economic achievement. It can even shorten our life expectancy. On the other hand, the absence of anger can lengthen our lives. Recent studies have found that having a positive mental attitude increases our average life expectancy by about seven and one-half years. So if you can expect to live seven years longer and feel better in the process, isn't that reason enough to learn to live without anger?

ANGER'S "POSITIVE" SIDE

Still, you might be protesting that anger has its positive attributes as well. And you're right. For one thing, it can motivate you to a higher level of performance. In an athletic event, for example, if you get mad at the other guy your adrenaline will increase, allowing you to put out the extra effort which could very well increase your chances of improving your normal performance. However, you could also achieve a peak performance just by wanting to do your very best. Experiencing what is called a "runner's high," for example, is the result of an adrenaline rush created by a positive emotion. So, which

motivating force would you rather use to achieve a peak performance: anger or the natural high that comes from the
desire to do your best?

Some feel that we need anger in order to respond most
effectively in some situations. For example, if you see someone beating a child, your anger gives you the energy and the
desire to respond. Many use anger to motivate themselves to
be more assertive. It's true that anger may be helpful in certain situations, but it's usually not the best way. You will be
more effective with a thought-out response. Anger can overcome fear, but response without reason can be disastrous.

Another "benefit" of anger? It gives us an excuse for our
bad behavior, just as alcohol does. We can blame our actions
on our altered state of consciousness and at the same time do
things we wouldn't have the courage to do were we not angry
enough. Just as some people will make allowances for others
who do violent or stupid things when they're drunk, there are
those who will make allowances for the things angry people
do. But do we really want to use our anger as an excuse?

THE COSTS OF ANGER

Anger exposes our weaknesses. It causes us to lose control and
to act in dogmatic ways. We make foolish decisions, we waste
time and energy, and we may become obsessed with our self and
the people we are angry with. We antagonize the people we love,
and we lose friends. We do crazy, destructive, sometimes illegal
things. We have stress, high blood pressure, intestinal problems,
heart problems, and other physical discomforts.

Anger and its expression do not exist on their own. Anger
always has a trigger, which we respond to by becoming angry

or not. Triggers are the things that will open up one of our memory files with which we have associated a strong negative charge (unpleasant memory). They are the things that happen that make us feel bad. For example, whenever someone is late for an appointment with you it may trigger a negative response.

In all areas of our lives, we make choices about how we behave. When we respond. How we respond. Whether or not we reveal our anger. Expressing our anger can often make the situation worse. But suppressed anger can also be bad, if by not revealing our feelings, the stress continues.

Our various inhibitions control the extent to which we suppress our anger. We have moral inhibitions because we learn to follow society's rules, and our own value system. We have practical inhibitions, because of what will happen to us if we express anger. We may get fired. Someone won't like us, or we may even get a bloody nose. Rather than suppressing and therefore holding onto our anger internally, the key is to find a way to release our anger.

A lot of work has been done in the field of anger management dealing with how to either manage our anger or how to release it. Releasing our anger is not only beneficial to our mental and physical health, it also allows us to operate more effectively in this society.

However, releasing anger is only the second best answer. When we learn how to never get angry in the first place then we are able to respond to life circumstances in our most efficient manner. And we never even have to face all of the problems associated with feeling angry.

Anger works to show other people they are out of order, but there are other ways to show people that we are unhappy with them. We don't have to use anger as a substitute for our lack of assertiveness. We can learn to be assertive without being angry. We will be much more effective and much happier when we do.

▲

EXERCISE
What Is Anger Costing You?

- List some of the relationships in your life that have been lost because of anger.

- List some of the goals you have not met because of anger.

- List some of the things you wanted but have not gotten because of anger.

EXERCISE
Understanding Yourself

- How often are you angry?

- Think about how you protect yourself by being angry.

- What are your favorite defenses?

- Make a list of the defenses you put up to protect your feelings.

- What are you afraid of that causes you to use these defense mechanisms?

EXERCISE

Anger Story

- Write out your own anger story.

- What are the things that make you angry?

- How intense is your anger?

- How long does it last?

- How do you express it?

- Do you think this anger is good to have?

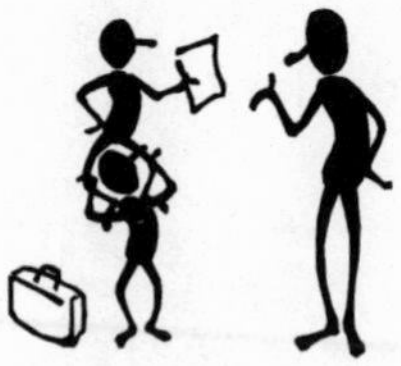

CHAPTER 8

The Case For No Anger

Once you decide to abandon anger, you will begin to enjoy a richer life and a host of benefits. Our ability to love, to be creative, to be at peace, to achieve our goals, and to enjoy our day to day living are greatly enhanced once we are no longer ruled by our anger.

What I want in my life is joy and happiness. Any time I am experiencing anger, I am not experiencing joy and happiness. Therefore anger detracts from my desire to live this life to the fullest. I am not moving toward my goal in life if I am in anger. If we value happiness, if we value joy, then we need to change our personal belief system to be aligned with that principle.

Anger and love are incompatible. The way to experience love is to let go of anger. Most of us spend a lot of time in anger, but the decision to get angry has powerful consequences. Once you make the decision not to get angry, you'll notice how the absence of anger will bring more love into your life.

You know what it is like to be around someone who blocks your life energy. That person is usually being negative in some way—the black cloud that hangs over an otherwise positive environment. When you are angry, you are doing the same thing to yourself. Negative (cold prickly) emotions drain our life energy. They rob us of our enjoyment of life. Our anger rarely has a positive effect on other people. As a result of our anger, we have less positive relationships. Our anger tends to prevent us from getting close to other people, because no one enjoys being around us when we are angry—unless they are angry about the same thing we are.

Learning unconditional acceptance of other people is a key to letting go of anger, and when we do so, it can greatly enrich our lives. We are each unique individuals, we come from different cultures and traditions, but we are also all human beings. We can be at peace with others and with our selves when we accept that. When we do, our feelings of love and friendship increase. Unconditional acceptance allows us to experience a more enjoyable, interesting, and rewarding life. When we give up feeling angry that others are not exactly like us, we feel at peace, and we're able to experience a much more satisfying life. When we embrace the world, it embraces us back. Recognize and respect the differences in everyone. Everyone has a different heart-song. Learn to sit back and appreciate the music. Learn to enjoy being one of the musicians.

A more creative life also awaits us when we abandon anger. Ford wasn't angry when he invented the assembly line. Edison wasn't angry when he invented the light bulb. If they were angry, those things never would have happened. When we are angry, we are no longer creative. Creativity is not found in our emotional center, but in the intellect and intuition. Anger interferes with efficient problem solving, creativity, accomplishments, and success seeking. It prevents us from using our best energy to accomplish all we want in life. Without anger we are able to put all of our effort into finding solutions. We are not inhibited by our sense of what should be. We are able to think outside of the box. We free ourselves from the limitations that inhibit our creativity.

Another benefit of a life without anger is the ability to appreciate the positive aspects of our life, rather than to be angry about the negative ones. Not only does this enrich our life because we feel positive nearly all of the time, it actually allows us to live a longer and healthier life

By eliminating anger, we enter a deeper state of calm and peace. In our inner being we really do want to achieve peace, and peace comes from letting go of anger and fear. Inner peace is a healthy choice. The principles in this book will help you to remove your anger so that it will no longer control you. Whether your anger is merely a mild annoyance, or an intensely felt feeling that frequently overtakes you, releasing it completely from your life will be one of the most rewarding things you have ever done. In fact, you will likely find yourself living in a world of joy.

SOME ADDITIONAL THINGS WE GAIN WHEN WE GIVE UP ANGER

Most of us want to be true to our real self, rather than to what the anger makes us want to do. The best time to deal with our anger is before it happens. When we learn to not experience the anger, we eliminate all of the problems it causes and the negative feelings that go along with them.

The weight of evidence shows that expressing anger serves to make it stronger. Not only does it make it stronger, it also establishes a habit of dealing with things in an angry way. When we do not respond to momentary irritations but instead distract ourselves with more pleasant thoughts, we will feel better faster and may well avoid a shouting match.

Remember, to a large extent we upset ourselves. We make a choice to be angry. It is not something that we simply must do or experience. It is not the circumstances that upset us, but how we view them. Since we choose to upset ourselves, we can choose not to be upset. We have a choice in the matter.

Even if you are unable to prevent all of your anger responses, you can, at the very least, raise your anger threshold. You will then not experience anger in many of the situations that made you angry in the past. Any reduction in the amount of anger in your life will certainly be helpful.

Even when you do feel anger, there is no need to express it. Expressing anger usually makes it stronger. We are generally better off giving anger time to dissipate instead of just acting it out. When you feel anger, give it time and the emotion will weaken, and it may go away completely. Then you will not have to regret tomorrow what you said today.

We definitely can reduce the negative charges on our files and reduce our cold prickly feelings and irrational responses. We have the ability to think, feel, and act differently. We were not born angry, it is just something we learned to do. We have choice and absolute free will as to how we choose to respond in each and every situation. We can choose to act differently than how we have always acted. We can change our thinking. Our emotional upsets include thoughts, feelings, and actions that we can observe and change. You can change, unless you think you can't. And until you think you can, you won't.

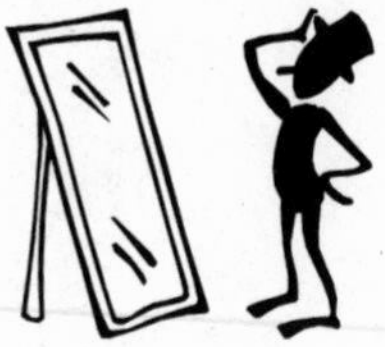

CHAPTER 9

Observing and Understanding Yourself

How do you go about changing yourself so that you will no longer experience anger? The first thing you need to do is to observe and understand what and how you think, and how you behave.

In order to know more about ourselves, we must develop the habit of observing how we react to all the messages sent to our brain. We can become observers of our own thoughts and actions so that we realize how certain thoughts trigger certain actions, and how those actions make us feel. This will allow us to know immediately when something has gone wrong—that is, when we are responding with anger instead of love. Observing our thoughts and actions will also give us some clues about how to fix them when they are wrong.

You can actually put a program in place in your mind that will function every time you open a mental file. This program will analyze the functioning of your brain by taking you through the following steps: Identify the message that came in. Determine which of your files you accessed with the incoming information. Notice how you processed the information once your memory files receive it. Notice what part of your brain processed the information. Notice how the information you already have stored in your file affected how you felt about the information you received. Notice what action you took and whether or not the outcome was as you would like it to be.

IDENTIFY THE MESSAGE

It is important to identify the sort of things that make you angry. Ask yourself what messages make you angry, and acknowledge that these are your anger "triggers." For example, an incoming message that triggers your anger might be: "I really get upset when someone doesn't put their dirty dishes in the dishwasher" or "I really get upset when my boss makes me work late."

DETERMINE THE "BELIEF" FILE YOU ACCESSED

Determine what it is in your belief and response system that produces the anger response. For example, your belief system may have included the following: "Everything must be orderly and neat" or "I do not do want to be late for dinner."

DETERMINE HOW YOU PROCESSED THE MESSAGE AFTER YOUR MEMORY FILE RECEIVED IT

What part of your brain processed the information? Your emotional center? Your thinking center? How did the information you already had stored in that file affect how you felt about the information you just received? For example, maybe you react with anger when things aren't as neat as you think they should be; or maybe you respond from both your emotional center and your thinking center when you find you will not be home for dinner as planned, because you know it will upset your family's plans as well as your own.

WHAT ACTION DID YOU TAKE?

What action did your angry response motivate you to take? For example, did you shout at your family for leaving the dirty dishes on the table? Did you tell you boss that he had no reason to treat you that way and he could just find someone else to do the job?

DID YOU FIND THAT ACTION HELPFUL OR NOT?

Notice whether or not the outcome of your action was as you would have liked it to be. For example, in the above situation, you might have felt that the action you took made you feel both upset and angry with everyone involved and really did nothing to solve the problem, because the dirty dishes were continually left on the table and your boss passed you over for the supervisor position you had hoped for.

COMPARE YOUR RESPONSE TO HOW YOU RESPONDED TO A SIMILAR PROBLEM IN THE PAST

Was your response appropriate for the present situation—or did you simply go into "automatic pilot" and use a response you'd used in the past because it was readily available in your "file" of responses? For instance, in the above examples, wouldn't it have been better to just leave the dishes on the table or put them in the sink yourself? Wouldn't it have gone better with the boss if you had said to him that you would like to help but had already made other plans with your family that were just too important to be changed?

Perception is not a fact. It is a mirror of our thoughts. No two people see the world the same. What you are doing in this process of observing yourself is finding out how you see the world. Try to see how your problems overlap each other and are inter-related. Try to see how your way of looking at things always agrees with your entrenched beliefs. Try to see how this way of thinking causes problems for you.

Especially pay attention to how you are feeling. "Emotional awareness" is being aware of what feelings are actually occurring in your body. Try to be more aware of your emotions and note how they make you feel. See if your responses are in line with the way you think and act during the times when you are able to respond without feeling the emotion. Notice how you feel about the things that happen, especially the events, statements, or behaviors that bother you.

Just the act of observing your emotions can take away some of the emotional charge. Watch what you avoid doing because the accompanying emotions seem unpleasant to you. Especially, notice when you are doing things that don't agree with your own thinking. When this happens, you are acting out of your emotional center. You need to make yourself aware of this so that you can determine why it happened, and what you can do to change your response the next time.

MAKING THE MOST ACCURATE CALL AS A SELF-OBSERVER

Although our objective is to be as rational and objective as we possibly can in observing ourselves, this is not an easy thing to do. We can liken this process to a controversial call in a basketball game. We tend to judge the call from the point of view of the team we are rooting for. Even though it may be difficult for us to see clearly what happened, we likely feel that any decision in favor of the other team was improperly made. If it goes our way, however, then we have no doubt that it was the right call. While we tend to use this kind of biased thinking in our own lives as well, we're now going to try to break that habit. When you are being the observer of your thoughts and actions, you are the referee, not the player or the fan. Your job is to be as objective as you can and to call them as you really see them. Be open to being wrong, but you have to believe that you have made the best call you could, and go with it. If your opinion proves to be wrong, be quick to recognize that and be willing to change the call. Be willing to make a different call the next time that you are faced with the same choice.

Remember, how you feel about what is happening depends on which side you are rooting for. Try to be objective, no labels and no judgments. Don't be tricked by your own prejudices and biases. Take the time to become aware of your own prejudices and biases so you will recognize them when they arise. It may help to ask yourself what are the other possible answers, or even, how would someone who has a different viewpoint see this event.

▲

EXERCISE

Discovering What Angers You

- For one week list each and every thing that made you angry or irritated.

- Note how you felt and what you did in response to what angered you. Also note how long you felt that way.

- Ask yourself how you could have better handled whatever triggered your anger.

- Ask yourself what you could have thought or done to not feel angry.

EXERCISE

Discovering The Things That Upset You

- For one week, note each and every time you complained about or criticized something.

- Note how you felt and what you did in response to what triggered your complaint or criticism. Was your response helpful? How important was it? Was there a better or more constructive way of dealing with the issue?

Note: When I first did this exercise, I was surprised to find that I was criticizing items in the evening news. I realized this was not the way I wanted to respond to what was going on in the world and knew I had something to change. Just identifying the problem was enough for me at that time. The change was easy, once I became aware that I had the problem. I decided that I was going to accept without judgment that this was simply the perspective of the news station with regard to what was happening in the world. Since I made that decision, I no longer experience those negative emotions when I watch the news.

EXERCISE
Listing Emotions

- List the warm fuzzys in your life.

- List the cold pricklys in your life.

- As you discover new emotional responses, add them to your list.

- With each one, ask yourself these questions:

- Who is associated with it?

- What is associated with it?

- What belief is causing me to feel this way?

- Do I want to hold onto this belief?

EXERCISE
Anger Story

- Write out your own anger story.

- What are the kind of things that make you angry?

- How intense is your anger?

- How long does it last?

- How do you express it?

- Is there anything about this anger that is beneficial?

EXERCISE
Anger List

- List all of the things that make you angry.

- List all of the things that make you irritated.

- List your pet peeves.

- Examine them.

- Make a decision to release those irritations that you are ready to release.

▼

CHAPTER 10

Changing Your Belief System

W e can change the world by changing our thoughts about it. When we learn to change the files that filter the input to our memories, we have the capacity to look at life—and everything that happens to us—differently. This process is referred to as changing our belief system. When we do this, we even change the system of cause and effect. How does this work? Once we've changed our view of the world, things will not work the same as they did before. Different responses will inspire different actions, which will in turn bring about different results. And this is the process by which we can rid ourselves of anger.

We feel the way we think. And we think the way we do because of our belief system. If we want to change the way we feel, then we must change our beliefs. You'll be the recipient of a wonderful new way of life if you can just alter your beliefs to encompass wonderful expectations of life. In other words, what you believe will happen is what will happen. Almost always, we find the world out there to be the world we expect it to be. So for the world to seem good to you, it is essential that you expect that it will be good.

We each have our own unique belief system, which is like a filter that new information passes through before it comes into our awareness. It is an extremely complex system that contains all of the things we have learned in life, beliefs that we have been taught and accepted as true. Our beliefs determine how we think the world works and embody the truths that we hold to be self-evident and accept without question. In order to make meaning out of any new input to our brains, we always compare it to our existing belief system.

Our belief system will always make perfect sense to us – at least until we are troubled by the answers we are getting and begin to re-evaluate them. This system is self-validating because it is *truth*, as we *believe* it to be. It is important to understand this if we hope to change the beliefs that trouble us. Understanding the nature of our belief system will help us to find the things we believe in that are not working for us, and that we may want to change. It will help us to change to more positive and effective beliefs.

And what is our ultimate goal in terms of changing our belief system? To intensify and deeply feel our positive emotions. Our goal is not to suppress our feelings in order to get rid of anger, because anger would still exist under the surface—demanding that we deal with it in another way. We don't want to suppress our feelings. We want to change them to different and desired feelings. Our objective is to fully experience our positive emotions. We want our love-based emotions to reach our feeling center and be fully accepted and acted on. When we filter the emotions coming into our minds, we want to have a system that will embrace the positive emotions. We make a choice about how we want to use the feeling center, and the most rewarding choice is to act out and feel love so that we can enjoy life more fully.

The basic rule is this: If your beliefs do not make you feel good, then they are not working right for you. They should then be evaluated for change. Open them up, examine them, turn them over, and determine if you want to keep them. Try to see why they are not giving you the results you want. Look for more effective beliefs to replace them with.

We are all doing the best we can in life. We follow our belief systems, until we realize they aren't working and need to be changed, and that we have the power to change them. When we decide that we can and do want to change a belief, it then becomes a matter of selecting a new belief and replacing the old one with the new one. We are learning to break our old habit by replacing it with new behavior that is more desirable.

It is not easy to change your way of looking at things. The first step is to identify the beliefs that are getting in the way of your major goals and the next is to decide what you want your overall perspective to be. Evaluate your whole belief system and see which beliefs are not working for you the way you would like. You can do this by pulling your beliefs out one at a time and looking at them. By embracing the ones that you want to keep, you make them stronger. Look for your irrational beliefs. Challenge the ones that don't give you good results, the ones that have negative emotions attached. For example, you may hold the belief that you should always defend your children's actions whatever the situation. Perhaps this has led you to defending your children when they are reprimanded by other people, which in turn has led you to get angry with a teacher or neighbor. If you were to change your belief system from "I should always defend my children" to " Let's try to find out what really happened here", you would be able to change your response from an angry to a civil one.

You can develop more helpful beliefs by changing the ones that routinely lead to angry responses. For example, instead of the belief that "Things should be the way I want them to be," a more helpful belief might be, "It will be nice if I can make things go the way I want, but if they don't I can still accept it."

If you want less anger in your life, think about incorporating new, less anger-producing beliefs into your belief system.

Examples of beliefs that do not produce anger:

- In the great scheme of life, this event is not all that important.

- Life is just as it is. I am not the boss of life.

- I accept ambiguity and uncertainty.

- I am open-minded; I am tolerant of others' ways and ideas.

- The goals that I am trying to achieve are just means, not ends.

- I am always open to creativity and originality.

- I take responsibility for my own direction in life.

- I accept any answer as possible, and possibly okay for others.

- I accept experimenting and risk-taking in myself and in others.

- I look to what is in my overall best interests for my life, not just what's best for today.

Trust the universe. Move from a closed to an open system when viewing the nature of life and society. Learn to take the world-view that all is one. See value in the points of view of others. Consider moderation, balance, and open-mindedness. A balanced view increases your choices. See values and events in life as gray instead of black and white. There is no one way of looking at things and no one right answer. Always be aware of that.

Look at your overall belief system. Is it based on love or fear? Which of your beliefs are fear or anger based? You become what you think you are, and the world becomes what you think it is. How do you see the world? How do you see yourself in it? How do you view your relationship with other people?

Remember that what we teach, what we do, what we practice is who we become. If we want to be free of anger we must think and act in accordance with beliefs that do not produce anger.

Guidelines to help you create a belief system that's free of anger:

- Choose to be caring of others.

- Do not see your interests as separate from other people's.

- Realize that being helpful and caring of others is in your own best interest—because you'll feel better and they will respond with love.

- Know that when you give love, love is returned.

Where do spiritual or religious beliefs fit into our discussion of beliefs that help us combat anger? Medical research has shown repeatedly that individuals who recognize a higher power have less stress-related illness, and thus less stress in their lives. Just having a central uniting theme or goal in life makes it easier to put our life into some form of meaningful order that we feel positive about. We must be aware of and learn to avoid a judgmental attitude toward our religious belief. When it comes to religious or spiritual beliefs, they must be accepted wholeheartedly. If you subscribe to a faith that you question or doubt, it can be a source of conflict and anger. We must accept the principles and beliefs of our faith to feel positive about it. And when we do, we are likely to feel less angry at the world because we feel more at one with ourselves.

Characteristics of a person who is one with himself/herself, and one with the world:

- They trust in themselves and in the universe.

- What they say, think, and do is in alignment.

- They are not judgmental.

- They are happy and are always expressing joy.

- They are not defensive.

- They give generously of themselves. Their attitude is: "How can I help?"

Work on changing your feelings and behaviors, as well as your thoughts. Making changes in your feelings and behaviors involves numerous thinking processes. You may need to make some deep philosophical changes in order to be the person you want to be.

Ask yourself, "What do I believe that makes me suffer?" Ask yourself, "How open is my belief system?" Choose to let go of every goal where your peace of mind depends on other people changing.

Here is something I keep on my wall as a reminder of how I want my world to be.

MY NEW BELIEF SYSTEM

- I want to believe that the world is fair.

- I want to believe that everyone is honest and good.

- I want to believe that anything is possible.

- I want to be oblivious to the complexities of life and be overly excited by the little things.

- I want to live simply.

- I want to believe in the power of smiles, hugs, a kind word, truth, and peace.

- I want to believe in dreams, imagination, humankind, and having fun.

- I want to embrace, accept, and enjoy the world.

- I want to love and be loved.

- I want to be remembered with a smile.

If some of these beliefs seem uncomfortable to you, try to determine why you feel that way. Look at the positive side of that belief and see how it could benefit your life. Pay attention to the beliefs you do accept. Work to align your other existing beliefs to be compatible with the ones you find acceptable. If your existing beliefs are in conflict, eliminate or modify the ones that contribute to anger. You create internal stress when your own beliefs are in conflict with each other.

▲

EXERCISE

Replacing Negative Beliefs with Positive Beliefs

• Identify which of your beliefs are anger-producing and therefore irrational.

• Refuse to accept your irrational beliefs.

• Determine the new belief that you want to put in its place.

• Use the program set forth in this book to create the new
belief.

> **NOTE:** Here we introduce tools for the first time. A tool is for the pur-
> pose of giving you something you can use continuously in your
> process of making changes in the way you respond to anger. If tools
> are helpful, use them; if they are not, or you need more, you can
> develop new ones of your own that work for you. Most of you will
> find many of these tools helpful in making desired changes in the way
> you respond to anger. They are designed to be helpful in developing
> new habits.

EXERCISE
Evaluating Your Beliefs

- What beliefs do you hold that are causing your anger?

- Do you want to get rid of the anger?

- What new belief could you put in the place of the old one to get rid of your anger?

- Can you accept this new belief?

- Are you ready to let go of the old belief?

TOOL
Changing Your Beliefs

- Using your tape recorder, state a belief that you currently hold but that you want to get rid of.

- Next, state the new belief that you want to replace the old one with, making sure that you state that you reject the old belief and accept the new one.

- Play the recording until you feel, and fully accept, the change in your beliefs.

TOOL

An Anger-free Role Model

- Locate someone who is a role model for behavior that reflects love, openness and creativity rather than anger.

- Find out what kind of thinking and beliefs are the foundation of their behavior.

- Ask them what benefits they derive from being free of anger.

- Ask them for suggestions regarding how to change your thinking.

- The next time you face an anger-triggering event, ask yourself how the role model would react in this situation—and model that behavior.

TOOL

Replacing Anger Responses

Any time you feel anger, or you have chosen the wrong response, review the event and decide how you would have preferred to respond. Practice this new behavior in your mind. Rehearse it and be ready to use it the next time the same or a similar situation arises. If your new response doesn't seem to be the one you want, select another one and try again.

TOOL

Acting Out New Beliefs

Write on 3 x 5 cards the old belief you had along with the new belief you want to put in its place. Then act out your new beliefs, being aware of the old belief that it is replacing each time that you do so. Keep rehearsing the new belief until it becomes your normal spontaneous response. Every time you revert to the old response look at the card and rehearse again.

▼

CHAPTER 11

Perception

Perception is the information that we input into our files, and it includes the choices we make about the information we take note of and the specific way we interpret that information. Since each of us sees life from our own frame of reference, our differing perceptions are often the source of conflict and anger. If we understand and choose to accept our differences, however, our dissimilar perceptions can become a source of wisdom, joy, and humor in our lives.

We tend to perceive information that supports the beliefs we have. First of all, we take note of the information presented to us that validates our belief system and often fail to notice things that do not. Next, we interpret the information that we receive in a way that is consistent with our existing belief system. What if this wasn't necessarily the case? What if we considered information in light of differing belief systems? And what if we always looked at things from a number of points of view before making a decision? In order to win a trial, lawyers are trained to carefully examine the other point of view. If they do not, they will not be prepared to respond with the best argument for their case. Likewise, you can learn to examine the information you receive from the points of view of all possibilities.

Which brings us to this key question concerning perception and anger: Do you want to be right or do you want to be happy? We know our opinions stem from our thoughts, not from external truth. So perhaps we shouldn't go to battle over our "truths" as we so often do. Although deeply held, your truths are not necessarily those of others. When you come to terms with this reality and place feeling good above the need to be right, you'll be taking a giant step toward eradicating the angry conflicts in your life.

The need to be right is also the need to prevail. We live in a competitive society, and we like to be winners. Part of being right is winning the conflict. Realize this, and know that your desire to be right is your ego trying to win another contest. Reframe your thinking to accept the idea that we are all in this together. Expect that others will think differently and that their perception of events will not be the same as yours.

So how might you change your way of looking at things to take into consideration someone else's perceptions—and to wind up with a more harmonious result? Imagine someone using a cell phone in a restaurant where you are having dinner. They're chatting away somewhat loudly, and this upsets you because you think they are making too much noise and being rude. But what if you came up with a new way of looking at the same situation—forced yourself, in other words, to perceive this unpleasant situation in a new, more pleasant light. That light might look something like this. "I'm going to imagine that this cell phone person is simply having a conversation with a real live dinner guest, and he is speaking as loudly as he is in fact speaking on the phone. I wouldn't be disturbed by that 'live conversation' scenario—so why should I be disturbed by his cell phone exchange?" In this example, by changing our perception of the event, we have succeeded in changing our response to it—from angry to accepting.

Another example of how easy it can be to change our perception is to take an optimistic viewpoint, one that leaves us feeling good. What if we were to change our viewpoint from "This is what I have to do today," to "This is what I would like to do today"? Our perception would change from a day ahead of us filled with obligation to one filled with positive promise.

A POSITIVE PERCEPTION

We need to learn to be for things that are positive rather than against the negative side of things. For example, we can be for peace, rather than against war. Being for something and working to achieve it is a positive experience. Being against something and fighting to bring it down is a negative, anger-based experience. You can work just as hard for your cause from the positive point of view as you can from the negative point of view. Even if you don't achieve any better results by being positive, you have prevented yourself from feeling the anger that comes from being against something.

Let us say for example that you are having a difficult relationship with your mate. If you work on the issues with the object of keeping the relationship together and it still fails, you will receive a lot of satisfaction just knowing that you did all that you could to keep the relationship together. You will be disappointed, but you will not be as likely to have a bitter feeling about the other person, because you have eliminated or reduced the bitterness of disagreement and anger.

Creating a more positive perception of a particularly difficult circumstance or event is always a choice we have. We can even choose how we perceive the severe adversities of life. Whenever you feel depressed, check to see how important the circumstance really is that's making you feel badly. Looking at the bigger picture helps us to realize that things may not be as bad as they feel at the moment. And even if they are, feeling bad about them is just going to get in the way of solving the problem and recovering from the disappointment.

Failure always gives us the opportunity to try something else. One of our greatest challenges is to learn to accept not achieving a goal. We can learn to look at such disappointments as a signal to re-evaluate our goals and as an opportunity to pursue different ones.

Our perceptions are not facts. They are mirrors of our thoughts in that we choose what to focus on, and our belief system determines how we interpret the information. The important thing to remember is that how we perceive a conversation with a loved one, the behavior of a friend, or our own personal performance depends on our unique frame of reference. If your perception results in a warm fuzzy, great! But if you're feeling a cold prickly, it is time to stop and review your perceptions and then try to determine why you are upset. If you want your perceptions to deliver different results, you must make some changes. Learn to accept a cold prickly as a signal that you may be in need of a "perception adjustment."

▲

EXERCISE
Compare Perceptions

With a friend, sit in a room or look at a picture of a room. Take thirty seconds to notice all the things you can about the room or picture. Leave the room or put the picture away. Each of you list on a piece of paper all of the items that you remember about the room or picture. Then write a description of how you would describe it. Next look at your lists and note the things that: 1. Were on both lists. 2. Were on one list. 3. Were on neither list.

Then discuss the differences in how each of you described the room. Discuss why you think that each of you:

- **Saw some things the same.**

- **Saw some things differently.**

- **Failed to note some things.**

▼

CHAPTER 12

——

Judgment

When I was young, I used to say that I felt like a gray person growing up in a black and white world. By that I meant that I could always see different viewpoints. It was never easy for me to make a decision because all of the alternatives had their merits. Choosing only one position or the other as my "one truth" was not comfortable for me. Although I may have had trouble making decisions at times, my natural inclination to reserve judgment and be open to many ways of thinking meant that I had little trouble with this particular aspect of anger. Because judging people as "wrong" can't help but make us angry.

Judgment is the decision that we make about the information that comes into our files. It is the decision that says to us, "This is what I believe based upon the information that I have received." Mostly we think of a judgment as agreement or disagreement with the information that we have received. But what is also included in a judgment are our existing beliefs and our own unique way of looking at things. In other words, judgments represent our assessment of the information that's been given to us, along with our beliefs, opinions, and perceptions.

Judgment comes from taking the things we perceive, processing them through our brain, and coming up with an answer. The judgment we make may be based on our emotions, our thinking, or both. We usually do not refer to it as a judgment if we still consider several possible answers or if we are not sure of the answer.

We think of judgment in terms of deciding what the answer is. Many of us have a real need to choose an answer, just because we are uncomfortable without one. When we judge we take sides, and we are always on the side which represents what we think is the right answer. But what if we could give up the need to choose sides and were able to look at an issue from all points of view? How might that affect our inclination to become angry?

HOW RESERVING JUDGMENT CAN LESSEN ANGER

One way to lessen our susceptibility to anger is to be open to the possibility of other "right" answers for ourselves and for others. Just accepting the possibility that the answer may change if we had more information keeps us open to the idea that the judgment we have made is only tentative and always subject to change. When we view a judgment in this manner, we don't have a strong emotional investment in it. And we find it easier to make changes when we receive new information that is not in agreement with our present way of thinking.

We all have separate realities, and when we honor the diversity that exists in the world and make our judgments accordingly, those whose views we may not share can complement our viewpoints and our way of doing things. We can give up the need to be right—and refuse to make judgments based on that need.

Sometimes you must make a choice because you must determine an action. Choose a response based on your best thinking, but don't place any emotional value on your choice. Don't take your truths too seriously. Always be looking for a better answer than the one you are acting on. When you see the possibility of a better choice, be open to changing your thinking. Rather than defending your original choice, see what you might learn by considering someone else's. Defending our choices, right or wrong, produces anger. Being open to differing choices produces solutions to problems. Another way we can learn to reserve judgment is to refrain from using words that categorize, evaluate, or judge.

Judgment Words to Avoid

- impossible

- can't

- try

- limitation

- if only

- but

- however

- difficult

- should

- disagree

We often use words that place limitations on our thinking and our available choice of solutions without even realizing that we're doing so.

If you expect others to conform to your judgments, you are doomed to failure, and this failure will invariably make you angry. There has never been anything that everyone has agreed on. Not only do others have a right to a different opinion, they most certainly always will. Anticipate and respect the opinions of others. Review them for any ideas that you may have not yet considered. Choose to let go of every goal where your peace of mind depends on other people changing. And give up the need to judge whether others are "right" or "wrong."

Don't try to change someone just because you can, or even because you feel you have the right to. First of all you don't, and second, you are not going to create a positive relationship with someone by trying to control how they should think and act. You have no more right to control another person's thinking and acting than they have to control yours.

Unfortunately, we often relate to each other as if we are to be constantly judged. We think it is important to decide who is wrong and who is right. We think that we need to be right. And if we are wrong, then we think we should suffer and be punished. If there is guilt, then we think there must be blame. We try to control someone else's behavior by placing blame upon them. Most of the time, we don't even realize that we do this. But if we are practicing guilt and blame, we see the other person as threatening us, so we attack them.

By learning not to judge others, we learn to accept ourselves. As long as we condemn others for their "mistakes," we will not be able to fully accept our own. We will be angry with ourselves because we are not living up to our own judgment of how we should be.

▲

EXERCISE
Avoiding Judgment

For one day, do not make any judgments. Any time you find yourself making a judgment, write it down. Ask yourself: Did I need to make this judgment? Was there a better way of looking at the issue? What other response could I have chosen?

TOOL
Reviewing Your Judgments

Take any judgment that causes you anger and review it. Ask yourself, "Why do I feel this way?" "How would I need to think in order not to be angry?" "Can I accept this new way of thinking as being valid?" "If not, then why not?" "Do I want to change my thinking, or do I want to hold onto my anger?"

If your choice is to change a belief then start that process of change.

AFFIRMATION

" I will judge nothing that occurs. I send love to everyone."

(Paste this on your mirror or use it as a computer screen saver.)

▼

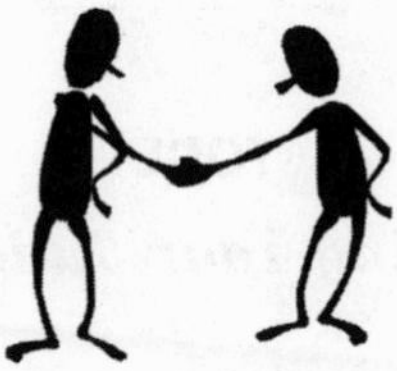

CHAPTER 13

Acceptance

Acceptance is what I call a judgment that is a warm fuzzy. It is a positive emotional choice. It is taking what the world has to offer you as being okay.

When we receive the circumstances that the world presents to us and realize that we can choose to just accept them as being so —we can eliminate a major source of our anger.

If we require a certain result, then we are addicted to the outcome. If we desire a certain result, we have a preference. If we have no preference as to what the results will be, then we are accepting. If we are accepting, then we have no negative emotions attached to the event or to the outcome. We can also learn that we do not have to be emotionally attached to the outcome, even when we have a preference. We can accept the idea that we are willing to try things the other person's way.

For everything that happens in our life, there are three possibilities: (1) We can change it. (2) We can leave it. (3) We can accept it. With each event, we need to make this choice. For example, consider your work. You may not be happy with it just the way it is. Is there a way you might change it to make it better? If that is not possible, then your next choice is to leave it. That may not be possible for the present, because you may need the work in order to eat or pay the rent. You then can choose to accept your work, or you may choose to make a plan to change to new employment in the future. If you choose to make a change later, then you need to make the decision to accept your work for now. As with all life experiences, if we don't find a way to make our work experience a positive one, then we are left with anger in our lives. To remove anger from your life, you need to apply this principle of "change, leave or accept."

For example, if there is something you really want to accomplish, give it your best. If you can't accomplish it—or if you're not willing to try hard enough to be successful at it—let it go and refuse to be upset by it any longer.

Accept your own choices and be happy with them. When you have made a decision, learn to accept it until you make a new decision to put in its place. You may need to change because you find the choice you made was not right for you. However, you can learn to develop an attitude that you are doing the best you know how for right now, and you will change whenever you find a better way.

ACCEPT DISAGREEMENT AND DIFFERENT PERSPECTIVES

We can accept disagreement without being disagreeable in return. We don't have to require that we be treated well. We can accept the way other people treat us, in the sense that we don't get angry about it. We can assert our boundaries and refuse to accept the other person's position, without being angry. If we believe in our self and our own truths, then we can let the other person have their own truths, and just refuse to be affected by them. If another person gives us a lot of cold pricklys, we always have the option of no longer having that person in our life.

Do we want to be happy, or do we want to be right? Whenever we are attached to being right, we are convinced the other person is wrong and we are right. As long as we cannot accept the idea that maybe they are also right, or at least realize that it just doesn't matter, we can't be free of anger or experience happiness and peace of mind. The more we accept the other person's reality as being authentic, the less angry we become.

As we become more accepting, we stop demanding that things go a certain way. It is a part of our nature to want to give and to receive love. When we demand things a certain way, we are not giving love, and we seldom get love in return when we do.

Accept that there are many vantage points from which to look at the same thing. You can change your way of looking at things to a way that is in line with happiness. The choice is yours.

ACCEPT OTHERS AS THEY ARE

Perhaps you're saying to yourself, "He is the one who makes me angry. I need to get him to change." This attitude is guaranteed to produce anger. If you can't accept your mate or your colleague or your child the way he or she is, your relationship is not going to be a happy one. This is something that we must do in order to have a rewarding relationship. Choose to let go of every goal where your peace of mind depends on other people changing. Learn to think, "I love you just the way you are."

ACCEPT YOURSELF

Give yourself unconditional self-acceptance. As you strive for your goals, acknowledge your own self-defeating ways and work hard to improve them. Accept your self as you are right now and as someone who is able to make any change that you truly desire, once you have decided to make the change. Whether you like the results or not, you are doing the best you can right now. Recognize that. Accept yourself fully for what you are now. You may want to change to something different, but for now this is where you are. Wanting to be different doesn't mean you are not okay for now – it's just where you are.

Challenge the "shoulds" and "must do's" in your life by believing that in the great scheme of things, this event is not all that important. Nothing is ever as important as it seems at the time. Try to remember that at the moment, if you can. If not, then take the time later to think about this.

ACCEPT THE GAME OF LIFE

All the stuff that happens around us is just the game of life. Accept it as such. Choose to play the game with warm fuzzys instead of cold pricklys—and learn to quit paying so much attention to things that tend to make you feel uncomfortable. Our most natural state of mind is contentment and joy. Believe that every experience is a positive experience in your life. It is at the very least a lesson that was helpful to learn. If we look at things this way, we can benefit from everything that happens to us. Be grateful for each life lesson, and for every opportunity to learn.

Cut some of the drama out of your thinking. You may be in the habit of thinking, "I can't stand it." But you can and you do. It is just an exaggeration. When we dramatize, we accelerate the stress in a stressful situation. We benefit by just accepting things, without adding to the problem by making them worse in our mind. We can add a lot of anger when we dramatize. Things we don't want to happen are going to happen. You will feel much better if you accept them.

Once you are fully able to convince yourself that you can stand whatever comes along, you will eliminate the horrors in your life. You will be left only with inconveniences, big and small. When we strongly believe that we can accept whatever comes into our lives, we no longer have a fear of the future. Our lives become serene and happy because we trust that we are our own masters. We can make the choices about how our lives go.

Remember: pursuits are not meant to be goals.

HAVE AN ATTITUDE OF GRATITUDE.

Be appreciative of what the world offers you. Be appreciative for what you receive from the world. Be appreciative that the world has so much abundance and *so many* opportunities for you to experience. You will not find happiness and joy without appreciation.

▲

EXERCISE
Making Choices

1. List all of the situations and relationships in your life that you are not happy with or which you would like to be different in some way.

2. Think about each one of these situations, and choose to change them, leave them, or accept them.

3. Make a plan for how to make the desired changes.

EXERCISE
Change Your Course by Accepting New Ideas

If you are feeling particularly angry or upset, reconsider the course you are on and give yourself some time to change it by doing the following:

1. Ask yourself, "What would my world be like if I unconditionally accepted myself and all others?"

2. Consider accepting: originality, self-direction, flexibility, risk-taking, experimentation, ambiguity, uncertainty, open-mindedness, tolerance, and not being attached to the outcome.

AFFIRMATION

"I accept what the world has to offer me. I have no complaints."

▼

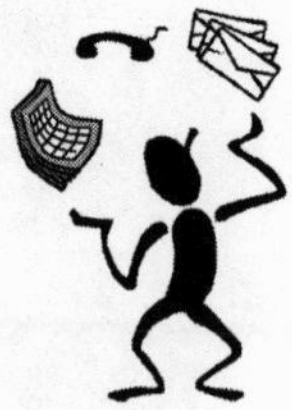

CHAPTER 14

Attachments

It is good to be attached to our positive goals. This attachment is part of the power that helps us attain those goals. Such attachment, however, should be limited to a continued focus on seeking your goal in a positive way. If this goal, or your pursuit of it, is no longer positive, then attempt to shift it back to being positive. If you can't, then release it. Seeking a goal that is no longer positive, or seeking it in a manner that is no longer positive, produces anger in our lives.

It is never good to be attached to our negative or hindering goals. As with our positive goals, our attachment creates the power to attain them. One of the skills we need to learn is to let go of those things that are cold pricklys in our life. Review your goals in all areas of your life and identify those that are upsetting you. Just like a smoker who would like to quit, we hang on to things that we think we just must have in our life, even though we know they are hurting us. Try to figure out why you are pursuing a negative goal so that you will gain new insight about your own motivation and therefore be able to let go.

When you identify an attachment you have that is not serving you well, treat it as an anger that you want to remove from your life. Use the same process for removing this attachment that you would use to remove the anger related to it. One of the greatest problems we humans experience is that we hang on to old attachments that no longer serve us, just because we have grown accustomed to them. Letting go is especially difficult when we have also grown fond of the old attachment. Review in your mind why you want to release an old attachment and remind yourself of that reason as often as necessary.

One of the most difficult lessons we have to learn is to let go of the past and to judge a situation based on its present merits. Something that worked for us when we were ten years old may no longer work for us today. When something becomes a cold prickly in your life, you need to take the time to open it up and examine it. Find what is causing you to feel that way. Decide whether it is something you can change, or fix in some way, in order to make it a warm fuzzy again. If it's possible, fix it. If not, then it is time to let go. Start the process of changing.

Once you have made the decision to let go of a negative attachment, the next step is to make the commitment to release it. Have faith that the attachment can be released. And finally, go through the work of breaking an old habit and putting a new one in its place. Some of us have the skills to let go of attachments quickly. For others, it can take more time.

How quickly you release an attachment determines how much pain you experience. Releasing an unwanted attachment will bring you back to joy and happiness. Realize that if you give up on letting go of the negative attachment before you finish the process, you will be back where you started.

You will still have the same old problem and will have to either live with it or start the process of change all over again.

Some people can release attachments by just letting go and moving on. Those of us who find it more difficult will benefit from finding a new positive interest with which to replace our negative attachment. To be free of anger, we need positive events and emotions to be the normal experiences in our life.

If you feel grief over relinquishing an attachment, recognize that it is a part of the process for many of us. Accept the sadness, knowing that you can move through it when you are ready. Do not accept the idea that there are rules about grief. They are just the guidelines about what most people in this society do. It is up to you whether you follow them or not. You are free to move at your own pace. Do not feel that you have any social obligation to act in a certain way.

Learn to embrace change. Your life has not been perfect. You can make it better by letting go of old attachments so that you can pursue more desirable goals. When something does not work the way you want it to and you can't change it, concentrate on replacing it with something new. Think of what you want in its place. This focus on the new positive goal is helpful in letting go of the old negative attachment.

You will find it helpful at this point to focus on the knowledge that you are now open to a new opportunity. This is the time that you can choose something new in your life. You want your life to be better. Choose something that will make it so. You may even find that it is time to train for a new career.

Just know that all negative attachments can be released, if and when you are up to doing so. If you are having difficulty letting go, the exercise in Chapter 30, "Releasing Old Anger", can be used to release attachments as well.

▲

EXERCISE
Old Attachments

Think about the things in your past that you were once attached to. Think about how you have moved on now that they are no longer in your life. Think about how you released the old attachment. Decide if you are happy with how you did it. If you are not, think about how you could learn to speed up or ease the process.

TOOL
Reminder Note

Make a note to yourself that states the desire to give up a specific attachment. Place the note on your refrigerator, mirror, or somewhere you will see it. It should read something like "I am no longer attached to _____."

AFFIRMATION
"I am not attached to the outcome."

▼

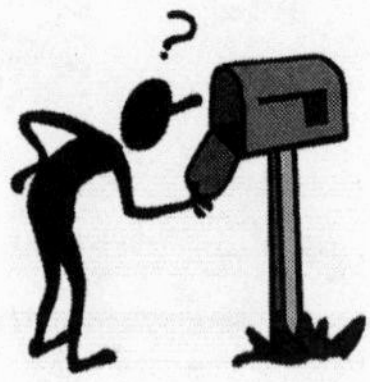

CHAPTER 15

———

Expectations

Everyone has expectations. They are at the very heart of being human. They reflect our ability to contemplate the future, to dream, to desire. Humans also have the ability to bring these expectations into reality. Why should anger be the response to the thwarting of expectations? We could choose to be amused when things don't meet our expectations. It is not the unfulfilled expectation that produces the anger; it is our interpretation of why the expectation was unfulfilled. We can look at it either as a personal affront or in some other way, such as the funny side of life. For most of the small indignities of life, we would be much better off just laughing at them.

Any time we set up specific conditions, expectations, or requirements for what must happen, or what we expect others to do in order to have happiness in our lives, we set ourselves up for anger. We are all unique individuals, and other people are not trained to, nor do they expect to meet, our every need. They are much more concerned with their own needs than they are with ours. Don't expect others to have known or done what you would have wanted them to. Don't get stuck in the "They should have...." trap.

Satisfying and positive relationships result from our mutual caring about and assisting each other, not from obligation. While others have no obligation to meet our needs, they often find that they benefit from doing so. When we help others, we often get much more in return. Being of service to others will provide much happiness. It will also remove many of the potential anger-producing situations from our life.

Too often we end up manipulating others to do things our way, without even realizing it. This creates anger because it's not what they want to do and they will therefore resist us. And this resistance will cause us both to be angry. This takes energy that could better be used in more constructive ways. Learn not to impose your own expectations on others. Learn not to expect from others. This is parallel to the victim role. Be your own person and honor the rights of others to be their own person. If you think that the world or some other person owes you something, then you have set yourself up for anger when the things that you think should happen don't. When we learn not to expect from others, we both end up being happier and more fulfilled.

Furthermore, the expectations of others are going to be different than yours, and to assume that they're the same will only cause you problems. We create conflict for ourselves all the time by assuming that others expect what we expect. This is especially obvious in a marriage. We often marry someone expecting that they will act according to society's accepted rules for marital partners, or in the same way our parents did, or that our marriage will resemble that of our parents in some general way. But we have no right to expect that someone live up to our expectations unless they agree to. Just because they marry us does not mean that our partner has agreed to do the cooking and the cleaning or to be the breadwinner. Anything you consider important in your marriage should be agreed to ahead of time. Remember that the customary ways that things are done in this society are just general rules and are only relevant to those who accept them. Don't fall into the trap of thinking someone should be a certain way just because most others are.

In dealing with others, the best rule is to start from a place of trust, realizing and accepting that you could be wrong. People tend to respond to you in the same way that you act. You will receive far more trust if you offer trust. If you offer distrust, that is what you usually get back. If you want to be free from anger, you will need to choose trust.

In dealing with problems that need positive responses, we are more effective (and feel better) being assertive instead of aggressive. When we respond from our thinking center, we choose a thought-out response rather than an emotional one. We can be assertive and accomplish what we feel we must without being angry. It is much easier to be assertive rather than aggressive if we have not set up some expectations that upset us when they are not met.

We need to learn to not let our peace of mind become dependent on what another person does. Except for adhering to the laws set down by our society, we have no right to expect that anyone act in a certain way, just as they have no right to require that from us. If you want to wash cars in return for your partner washing shirts, and they want the same deal, that is great. However, if this arrangement isn't okay with them, then find another solution, even if you have to wash your own shirts or take them to the laundry.

We tend to place a lot of value on our expectations. If it is important for you to be right, then you will find yourself needing to fulfill your expectations. But if it is more important for you to be happy, you will accept what is happening. You will be looking for the most effective response, rather than the response that best fits your expectations.

What we expect is exactly what we get. We can change our thinking from "This is what I have to do today" to "I am looking forward to what is happening today." Your attitude and your behavior will change because you have changed your expectations of how you see the day unfolding.

EXERCISE
Working Out Differences

Sit down with your mate or any person with whom you are having a relationship problem. Discuss what you would each like to see happen. Work out a plan by which you resolve your differences in a way that makes you both happiest. Understand that it may take some serious compromises on each of your parts. Be willing to look for non-traditional solutions. Acknowledge how this plan is far superior to simply expecting something from each other.

CHAPTER 16

Victim Thinking

In this world, many unpleasant, distasteful, even tragic things are going to happen, and some of them are going to happen to you. Whether or not you are a victim does not depend on what happens to you. It is determined by what you think – by how you respond. Whenever you give someone the power over you in some way, you are choosing the victim role.

Most of us play victim roles all our lives, because that is what our society teaches us. We have a society that assigns people to positions of power and teaches that power is strength and a good thing to have and use. Such thinking is how our society keeps people under control. It creates a system whereby the strong tend to make the rules in a way that keeps those who are willing to be victims under their control. Most of our advertising is based on the concept of appealing to our victim attitude. Advertisers try to make us feel we need their products in order to feel whole. If we don't use their products, then we must be inadequate.

ARE YOU THE VICTIM OF YOUR OWN THINKING?

We also tend to make ourselves the victim of our own thinking. We grow up expecting certain things out of life, and when those things don't happen, we feel cheated. When something bad happens we tend to say, "What did I ever do to deserve this?" We find it difficult just to accept what happens because we get tied up in our own expectations and attachments.

We put ourselves in the victim role whenever we deny that the feeling of being a victim actually originates in our own mind. If you find yourself thinking in terms of "How can I possibly cope with this awful situation?" you are admitting that you are a victim. Thinking about how you can just "get by" is victim thinking.

Instead, we need to think in terms of , "I am in control here." "I am the boss of me and my life." Until you take over the control of your life in every way, you are making yourself a victim. Taking control means that you are the one who makes the choices about your own life based on your independent needs and thinking. It means that you are not making your choices based on what someone else is telling you that you must or must not do.

Refuse to become the victim of your own beliefs. If you have beliefs that depreciate or upset you, dispute them. Any time one of your beliefs is bothering you, examine it.

If you think you may be a victim of your own beliefs, ask yourself these questions:

- Where is the evidence that this belief is true?

- Do I hold this belief based on my own independent thinking?

- Will this belief help me in my life?

- What has this belief done for me so far?

- How will this belief likely affect me in the future?

- How does it fit in with my other beliefs?

- Is there a better belief to replace it?

CHANGE SHAMED TO SORRY

Do not be ashamed of yourself. You are always doing the best you can at the moment. You can be sorry for the effect your action had on other people and can decide to change your behavior in the future, but when you feel ashamed you make yourself a victim of your own feelings. Any time that you are angry with your self, you become the victim of your own thinking.

HOW MOODS AFFECT VICTIM THINKING

Sometimes we feel much stronger, much more positive, much happier than on other occasions. Moods are part of the human condition. Learn to question your judgment when you are in a low state. Remember that you didn't feel the same way yesterday. Understand the power of your moods. Learn to accept them as the way you feel at the moment. If you learn to respond from your intellect rather than your feelings, you will move through your mood much more quickly because you will not compound the problem with emotions that aren't relevant to what's actually going on.

Moods are one of the core problems in relationships. The trick is to recognize the state of mind you are in. Once you recognize that you're in an angry, sad, or otherwise negative mood, you can then take it into account as you make your decision regarding how to respond. Moods can't be maintained over long periods of time; they always pass. The trick is to not let them mess up your life while you are feeling them. Postponing responses will be helpful in many instances.

Recognize when you are in a low mood. Recognize when you are emotional. Have a set response for when you are. Be able to sense and understand a low mood in others. You can respond differently, respecting how the other person is feeling and with an understanding of why it is happening. When you are emotionally disturbed, you have harmful negative thoughts. You may often have strong faith in those thoughts. Learn to recognize when they are coming from a mood that you know will pass and postpone placing value on them.

BREAK OUT OF THE "PASSIVITY PRISON"

If we took responsibility for our feelings, no one would ever feel like a victim. When something doesn't go our way, we would not think, "poor little me." Helplessness and despair arise from feeling like a victim, and feeling like a victim gives rise to anger. If something is broke, fix it, don't complain; solve your problem. If you can't work because you have a bad back, get the training so you can do something that a bad back will not prevent you from doing.

Break away from the passivity prison. Nobody likes to be a victim, afraid of making a decisive move. If you find a decision difficult to make, give yourself time to get the input you need, make a choice, and move on. Be open to change again if you see you have made the wrong choice. Don't try to live with your mistakes – correct them. If you are unable to make choices, then you are the victim of your own thinking.

As you learn to ask yourself, "What can I do to improve this situation?" rather than "Why did this happen to me?" your perspective will shift from being the victim to being the problem-solver. Start thinking of yourself as being capable of solving problems. Know that all problems have potential positive solutions. Enjoy the search for them. You will delight in the results that come from finding answers.

▲

EXERCISE
Examine Your Victim Beliefs

1. List the things in life that you think are unfair.

2. List the things at work that you think are unfair.

3. List the things at home that you think are unfair.

4. List the ways you think others are not fair with you.

5. Now take each of these items and try to analyze why you think it's unfair.

6. Ask yourself what you can do to change it.

7. If you choose to do nothing to change it, consider accepting it.

▼

CHAPTER 17

———

Humor

Humor is another filter file that you will want to use as often as possible in order to eradicate the anger in your life. When we look for the humor in every situation and respond with humor whenever possible, we tend to blunt the existing negative charge on a mental file and instead put a positive charge on it. By doing this, we create warm fuzzys.

Humor can also be thought of as a way of re-appraising a situation. Because you have thought of something in a humorous way, you have put a positive charge on it. You have intentionally placed yourself in your positive emotions when you choose humor as a response. Also, you send the information from your emotions to your intellect in order to develop an effective reply.

When you respond with humor, you are often able to actually change what would have been a cold prickly into a warm fuzzy.

By using humor, we're telling ourselves that we refuse to take things too seriously. Humor reduces the seriousness of your thoughts. It shows that you can laugh at your failures.

Humor laughs at your failures, but in an accepting and tolerant way. It helps you see another side of things. It reveals to you that, whatever misfortune or catastrophe has landed on your doorstep, it's not the end of the world. Humor is a love-based emotion. When you use it, you avoid feeling negative emotions.

Speakers invariably use humor to get the attention of their audience. They do this because of its powerful positive effect. Because most people like to laugh, humor tends to get the other person to accept what you are saying or doing in a positive way. When you use humor, it creates a positive feeling for your ideas in the hearts and minds of others. When used effectively, it is a powerful—and wonderful—tool.

When using the humor file, there are some guidelines you should follow in order to make its use more effective:

- **Consider what your humorous response does for you.** Does it defuse a negative emotion? Does it move you into positive emotions just because you enjoy your own humor?

- **Consider how your humorous response will affect the other person.** Their response reaction will affect you. If it is positive, it will defuse the situation, but if it is negative it can make the situation worse. If you offend the other person, you will end up making things more difficult for yourself. Be aware of what kind of humor is acceptable.

LOVE-BASED VERSUS ANGER-BASED "HUMOR"

Sarcasm isn't humor. Sarcasm is based in anger and will usually elicit an angry response from others. The same is true for any so-called "humor" that invalidates or depreciates another person or group of people or the deeply held values of others. Such anger-based humor feeds your own biases. We learn to use this kind of response when we are growing up. Children learn to use sarcasm and "humorous" put-downs as a way of having power over others. Making fun of others is used intentionally to produce anger. If you want power over others, use sarcasm. If you want to move beyond anger, avoid using sarcasm.

The key to knowing how to tell love-based humor from anger-based "humor" is this: If it's disrespectful toward another person or group of people, it is not love-based. On the other hand, when you laugh with others about your own shortcomings, it is much more difficult for them to laugh at you. It is also more difficult for them to be angry with you. By having a friendly and funny response that is not disrespectful of the position of the other person, you will be encouraging them to be friendly and positive as well. By laughing with others and at the situation, you are refusing to play the victim role.

WHY HUMOR REDUCES STRESS

Humor is a good way to divert your attention from a stressful situation so that you can more easily accept and deal with it. You experience what you are focusing on. With your focus on humor, you are focusing on positive emotions. The anxiety of anticipating something negative is greatly lessened by focusing on the humor. When you anticipate the stress, you then feel the pain. The basic rule is that what you dwell on becomes yours. Joke with the dentist when he is pulling your tooth, and you will have less pain. The story of Doctor Patch Adams and how he uses humor in healing his medical patients is a great example of what humor can do for us.

We use humor all of the time in our society as a way of deflecting the stress and anger in our lives. The reason why the best professional comedians are so popular and well respected is that they have had a powerful positive effect on our lives. Erma Bombeck, Robin Williams, George Burns, Lucille Ball, Bill Cosby, and many more have become immortal because they help us see the world's problems and our own—including the things that make us so angry—in a new light, a laughable light. When you learn to use humor as part of your way of thinking and responding, you will provide these great benefits to yourself.

You can view life as either a tragedy or a comedy. This doesn't mean that you have to be the good humor man and always be laughing out loud and telling funny stories. It means that whatever happens in your life, you will tend to smile or laugh, rather than look on the dark side. Make the choice that life is fun and live it that way.

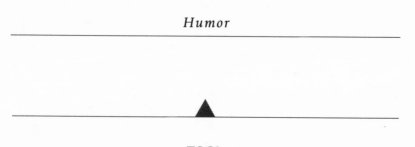

TOOL

Read the Comics

Each morning, take some time to read the comics. Enjoy the humor. Accept this as a good way to get you in the right attitude to enjoy the day. Whenever you find yourself in a waiting room and the least bit apprehensive, pick up a copy of the Reader's Digest. Flip through it and read the humor. This will help to defuse your anxiety. Take the opportunity whenever you can to look, read, or listen to humor—and take the time to appreciate it. Make it a practice to tell others about the things you see that are especially funny to you.

TOOL

Laugh Out Loud!

When you are feeling in a low mood or are disturbed by some situation or event, take the time to laugh. Laugh at yourself for feeling that way. Laugh out loud until you no longer feel upset. Find a "laughing partner" or join a "laughing club." You can try laughing at yourself in the mirror. Although you may find it awkward at first, laughing out loud is a powerful anger-buster!

AFFIRMATION

"I find humor in everything I see."

CHAPTER 18

Forgiveness

Have you ever asked yourself, "Why can't I forgive that person? Why can't I forgive myself? Why can't I let go of old anger and forgive?"

We can always come up with a reason why we should not forgive. The most common one is: "It was their fault. They deserve my anger." (Or, "I'm to blame—how can I ever forgive myself?") Our society teaches us that people should pay for their mistakes. This comes from the ancient idea of "an eye for an eye." We have been taught that when we are wronged, we must punish the wrongdoer, that "Such behavior just cannot be tolerated—you will pay for it" and "The guilty must be caught and punished." Raised with such societal beliefs about guilt and punishment, we think we must make others suffer, as punishment for having offended us. We believe we must return the hurt to get even. But thinking in this way is really more of an emotional response than an effective thinking response that allows us to maximize our life experience.

Some one may have killed a loved one of ours in an unfortunate automobile accident. Regardless of whether it was carelessness or not that person's fault, we find it difficult to forgive them. If you cannot forgive, that person now has the power over you. He is affecting your life. As long as you hold the anger, you are continuing to be hurt. This is a bit like being sick and saying to the doctor, "I want to keep this pain, so please don't make me well." The lesson is that forgiveness is for our own benefit and has nothing to do with what the other person did.

Forgiving does not mean condoning the behavior. Even though you may have been cheated or hurt in some way, it is still appropriate to forgive. Forgiveness has nothing to do with right or wrong. Forgiveness is letting go of hurt from the past. Unfortunately, we learn from society and from our families that not only is it okay to hold grudges, it's appropriate to do so. But hanging on to old anger prevents us from enjoying our life and can even make us physically ill. We live longer and better when we are able to forgive.

When we can learn to view the people whom we want to forgive as acting only in the ways they were taught or in the only way they know how, then it is much easier to forgive them. Realize that what someone did to hurt you was usually done out of fear and confusion, not as something having to do with you personally. Their actions arose from their own fears and the ways they have learned to deal with things. You became the object of those fears and that confusion because you happened to be there. Have compassion for the problems you realize such people have; this will make it easier to forgive their acts.

FORGIVENESS LEADS TO PEACE OF MIND

Holding onto anger and grudges wears us down, both physically and mentally. Tests show huge increases in heart rate, blood pressure, and muscle tension when people are thinking about old angers they have not forgiven. Forgiving, on the other hand, improves your overall health and length of life.

Forgiveness allows us to stop re-running anger and blame. As long as we hold on to those, we keep replaying them. If we hold on to what causes pain, then we cannot practice any of the methods that can heal. Forgiveness is one of those methods, one of the spiritual acts that brings an end to our inner conflicts.

To be happy, we must be able to forgive others, and to forgive others we must first learn to forgive ourselves. If we blame ourselves for our mistakes then we will hold others at fault for theirs. Realize that people make mistakes all the time and that you and they are only human in that regard.

We learn from all spiritual teachings that to err is human and forgiveness is divine. The Christian scriptures remind us that we are to forgive others the same way God has forgiven us. We often seem to mouth these lessons without fully absorbing them.

You either totally forgive or you don't forgive at all. Sort of forgiving doesn't work. Make peace of mind your only goal. Rather than being angry, mournful, or upset at a relationship that has ended, for example, be thankful and appreciative for what you once had. Enjoy the memories as you also look to your future. Longing for a return to the relationship is not helpful unless that is a possibility. If you are having trouble forgiving unjustified losses, you may want to review the chapter on Attachments.

Forgiveness is:

- Accepting the fact that a mistake was made and moving on.

- Correcting your perception that the other person's behavior is the cause of your anger.

- Not requiring that the other person pay for your feelings.

- Not wanting to hurt the other person because they hurt you.

- Giving love where hatred is expected.

- Not allowing anything to hinder a relationship.

- Practicing unconditional love.

Forgiveness is not:

- Simply forgetting what happened.

- Pretending that everything is all right.

- Feeling that things will work out, or that things will get better if we leave them alone.

- Comforting yourself with the fact that God will get retribution.

- Just not bringing up the past.

We feel upset when we don't deal with unfinished business from the past. As we continue to hold onto our anger, our unforgiving thoughts become the cause of our suffering, and we continue to hurt. The only remedy for this pain and resentment is forgiveness. We can be free of suffering by letting go of the past. Becoming a happy person is really not possible until you free yourself from your anger and forgive.

If you find yourself fearful that what has happened in the past will happen in the future, try taking the opposite attitude—that things will be better now that you have learned the lesson inspired by the negative experience. Which attitude is the most productive—holding onto the anger and being miserable, or practicing forgiveness and learning from the experience? Why not consider the person who "wronged" you as a teacher? If you look upon them as a teacher of one of life's lessons, it will be much easier to forgive them. Be thankful for the lesson. View the situation from the perspective of how you dealt with it rather that what was done to you.

To decide not to forgive is to decide to suffer. By shifting your perspective and refusing to blame others or to carry any resentments, you open yourself to a happier existence. Forgiveness is letting go of all hope that we can somehow fix the past. We have all been hurt by the actions of others. It is always easy to justify our anger, but even with the strongest of justifications, you will never be happy if you hold onto it. The anger will have won out, and you will have lost, no matter how strong your "case." It will help you to forgive if you take the position that, in your life, no anger is justified.

Make the Decision to Find No Value In:

- Self pity

- Being a faultfinder

- Punishing your self

- Punishing others

- Being unhappy

Enjoy the happiness and peace that come with forgiving. Once you feel how good forgiving has made you feel, it becomes easier to do.

Forgiving is a continuous process. Old hurts that we have not fully forgiven will continue to come up. We will face new challenges frequently. Once we have made the decision to forgive, we have work ahead of us. Be ever watchful. When you find something or someone you have not forgiven, focus on it until your forgiveness is complete. Once you have made the decision to forgive, you will find forgiveness becoming easier and easier.

▲

EXERCISE
Forgiveness List

Make a list of grievances that you have with:

1. Parents, spouses, ex-spouses, family members, and relatives

2. Authority figures

3. Your superiors at work

4. The accidents and misdeeds of strangers

Once you have made this list, take the time to think carefully about each grievance until you can fully forgive each and every person on the list. Add new people and events to the list as you become aware of them.

EXERCISE
Forgiveness Letter

- Write a letter to the person you want to forgive.

- Forgive them.

- Do not mail the letter unless you honestly believe that either the relationship or the other person will truly benefit from it. Most likely you will not want to send the letter.

TOOL
Peace of Mind

To enhance your peace of mind, go out into nature, find a place to sit and reflect on the future. Think about how good life could be and what you have to forgive to get there.

▼

CHAPTER 19

Behavior

O ur own thinking about a situation creates our anger. Knowing this will help you to gain control of your anger. Since you created it, you can be in control of your anger. You can change your behavior so that you respond to anger-inducing situations in a new, more effective way. Realizing that your anger is your own creation makes it easier for you to change the way you respond.

A crucial part of dealing with anger is learning a new way to respond to situations. If you are flying an airplane and an engine fails, you have been taught how to get it started again, and if you can't, how to get onto the ground safely. You apply the emergency procedures you have learned. You never get angry, because you are too busy thinking about the problem. You can use a similar problem-solving strategy to deal with the anger that arises in any situation. When faced with such a situation, the key is to choose a behavior that is not controlled by your negative emotions.

TRAIN YOURSELF IN A NEW BEHAVIOR PATTERN

Changing a behavior pattern comes from training. All skills and professions teach this. However, most people have never learned how to avoid anger or how to behave when it does occur. That is what you are learning now.

You can make your behavior what you want it to be, rather than what others want it to be. If you don't choose your own behavior, you are probably not going to be happy with it. Learn to choose the behavior that you want to use, rather than what you think will make your friends or family happy.

Let's say that getting someone to pay back a debt is particularly anger-producing for you. If collecting the debt is unpleasant for you, allow yourself to avoid anger by not collecting it. If *not* collecting the debt is what makes you angry, allow yourself to collect it. If both actions are unpleasant, then you have an issue to deal with. You need to make a choice about how you wish to respond to situations like this in the future, based on which action leaves you feeling anger-free. Choose a response that feels good to you. Choose a warm fuzzy not a cold prickly. Don't choose the response simply because that was how you were taught to deal with the situation. If being effective is important, then find an effective response that feels good. For example, you might say to the other person, "It is really important to me that I get this money. Can you help me by repaying this debt?"

As you plan your new behavior in response to anger-inducing situations, think about what may transpire. Learn to not trap yourself in situations in which you have no satisfactory choices. If you have loaned someone money and you find it too unpleasant to collect it from that person, but you simply can't do without the money , you have put yourself in a position where you have no satisfactory choice. Learn to think through the possible consequences before you take action. This will avoid much anger-producing stress.

Most of us want to be true to our own belief systems. We want to respond the way we believe we should, rather than how we feel at the moment. Learn to follow your positive impulses in responding to situations. If you try to respond the way you *think* others want you to respond, you will find it more difficult to feel good about yourself.

You must learn to be in control. If you whine about something, you have chosen that behavior. Work at seeing how self-defeating it is to whine about things. Keep looking for the times you complain about things. Refuse to accept that behavior from yourself. Change your complaining attitude to one of observing and evaluating what is going on. The only thing you change by complaining is how you feel, and how others feel about you.

Avoid over-generalizing; it can feed a very defeatist attitude. For example, "Since I keep failing to get a job I want, I know I'll never get a job I want." "No desirable positions are available." "I had better give up and stop trying to get a good job and just settle for whatever I can get." Your over-generalizations are illogical and self-limiting. They will affect your thinking and your actions. Check and revise them.

Also avoid labeling, both other people and yourself. Rather than thinking "I'm lazy," why not think, "I don't feel like doing this thing at this time." You become what you think you are. When you choose positive things to think about yourself, you will be a positive person.

Challenge the shoulds, oughts, musts, and have-to's in you life. If you feel that you have to do something that you really don't want to do, then you are sure to get angry. If you really think it is the right thing to do, then just accept it and do it. If you think it might not be what you want to do, then think it through clearly, make a choice, and accept your choice.

It is self-defeating not to like the action you have chosen. This is a time to remember that you and only you are in control of your life. Once you make a choice, work to make it the right choice. If you find that it is not the right choice, then change it to a new and better choice.

Try not to dramatize your frustrations. Stay as close to reality as you possibly can. Give yourself time to respond. Don't allow your anger to dictate what you should do. If you can't get rid of the angry, frustrated feeling, divert yourself by doing something else until the feeling goes away.

This reminds me of going to the dentist. I used to be stressed out just anticipating the pain. And when I did, I always found that it really hurt. One day I said to myself, "If I don't anticipate it, at least it won't hurt until it actually does." And sure enough, it didn't. I had previously had some very painful experiences with the needle. I would tense up and it would hurt something terrible. Then I listened when the dentist said "relax." When I did relax, the pain was much less. I was able to stand it with little difficulty. Life in general is pretty much like that. If we accept what comes along, it won't hurt nearly as much as if we worry about it. Things happen; we had better learn to tolerate them happening.

The behavior we exhibit toward another person will affect their emotional charge, which will change their response to us. This will, in turn, change our emotional charge because we will not be as threatened by them. In this way, a previously tense situation can be totally diffused.

The opposite of aggression is not passivity. To not respond with anger does not mean not to respond at all. You don't need to be passive to avoid anger. Learn to be assertive, and state your position clearly and strongly. You can do this from your thinking center. We do not have to act out of our negative emotions to make our point or to do what we think is the right thing. Being passive and not asserting ourselves, is a sure way to invite anger.

Some people confuse being kind with being passive, but these attitudes are not at all the same. Being passive is just going along with what the other person wants you to do. Being kind is to consider the feelings and needs of the other person. We can assertively state our position with full consideration of the other person and their needs, thus showing kindness and friendliness. The only caveat is that you make sure that what you are doing or saying is exactly what you want in your life, including the affect your behavior has on other people. You can learn to be assertive and be just what you want to be without ever experiencing anger.

We can be assertive and still be kind. What is unkind is to mislead or to let the other person down. Be what you have led them to expect you are and be nice about it. They will have less anger, because they know just what to expect.

For example, when I was an aircraft commander, I did not have to be angry to be assertive. Anger would reduce the effectiveness of the response to my command. An emotional response to my command was less effective than a response to the urgency of my message from the other person's thinking center. An emotional response would be less effective in handling the situation.

Helping others is a behavior that generates a great deal of positive emotion. It makes you feel better about yourself both physically and emotionally. Always be open to being of service to others. Develop the attitude of "How can I help?"

When you realize that you have a habitual way of doing something that is anger producing, give yourself the benefit of engaging in another behavior that will distract you until you get rid of this bad habit in your life. The best way is usually the positive way. Find a new and exciting interest to take its place, and the old behavior will be much easier to eliminate.

Learn to avoid behaviors that cause you to become angry. Just as alcoholics learn that they must stay away from alcohol completely, if they do not want it to destroy their life, make sure to avoid the behaviors that cause you to get angry. For example, give yourself plenty of time to get to an appointment, if you know that being late makes you angry.

One way to replace old behavior is to visualize and imagine the new behavior that you want to take its place. Picture the new behavior. See yourself doing it until it becomes easy. For example, rather than losing your temper when your son tells you he has forgotten to study for his test, why don't you practice over and over in your mind explaining to your son the consequences of failing to study. Also consider a method he can use to study, so that it won't be something he tends to avoid. Practicing what you will say to him in this way will result in your being prepared the next time the studying issue comes up. This is a bit like a golfer practicing her golf swing over and over in her mind.

Angry behavior is not an effective way to deal with things. It is just going to make your life more difficult and unpleasant. It is time to realize that angry behavior is only the way you have chosen to respond, and that you can change your behavior any time you wish. Now is the time to evaluate and change your behavior using the skills and procedures presented in this book.

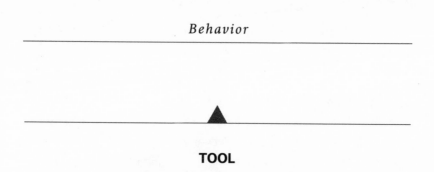

TOOL

Don't Be A Target for Anger

Don't let yourself be a target for other people's anger. Mentally stand sideways and let the angry "stuff" go by you. Picture yourself as standing out of the way and letting the anger fly by.

TOOL

Disconnect Your Anger Buttons

Imagine that you are wearing a breastplate full of buttons. If people "push your buttons" and activate your anger, change your response by deactivating your buttons.   Disconnect the button in your imagination.   Then, if someone pushes this button, it won't work. Remember that they will probably try another one. You can learn to deactivate your buttons ahead of time so that you are ready when someone tries to push one.

TOOL

Flack Jacket

When you feel threatened, put on a mental "flack jacket" so that you can absorb the anger producing thoughts that people are throwing at you.   Then you won't get angry because their message can't get to you. If someone says something that would otherwise disturb you, just imagine that you are wearing the jacket so that what they say doesn't get to you. (As an alternative, you may want to use a "mirrored jacket" instead—so that whatever is aimed at you goes right back to the sender. Use this jacket if it is a more comfortable image than a flack jacket.)

TOOL
Time-Out

If you feel a need to get away to reflect and think about what is happening, because you are too much in your emotional center, you can take time-out. If you are not interacting with another person, this is simple to do. However, if two or more are involved, do it tactfully and by agreement as much as possible, and always make an agreement about when you are going to get back to the issue.

TOOL
Get Physical

Engage in some aerobic exercise of your choice. It changes brain chemistry and reduces your emotional level.

TOOL
Self-Talk

Talk to yourself about what is going on and what you are feeling. Accept your failure. Give yourself strokes for your successes. Then move on to changing your behavior. Work with the things that bother you until you develop a new, anger-free behavior.

TOOL
Relaxation

When you feel stressed, emotional, or are experiencing cold pricklys, take the time to do some sort of relaxation exercise. You can do deep breathing, visualize a favorite place, listen to music, take a hot bath, or whatever works well to relax you. When you feel the need to relax, do so. Don't put it off.

TOOL
Practice Response

You can decide ahead of time what behavior you want to respond with. Think it through. Decide how you want to respond. Rehearse your response and then apply it when the situation arises.

You can first practice this way of responding in situations that only make you slightly disturbed. Broaden to those that are more difficult as you master this technique.

TOOL
Ban Angry Language

Eliminate all aggressive, inflammatory language (SOB, jerk, idiot, fool, etc.) whenever you communicate your feelings to others.

Refuse to criticize or complain about others' behavior. Most people fall into the habit of criticizing or complaining as a part of normal social discussion. Watch for this and train yourself not to respond or agree with them. Make an effort to change the discussion to positive thinking.

▼

CHAPTER 20

_____

Changing How You Process Incoming Information

A t this point in the "Life Without Anger" program, you have armed yourself with the knowledge and the tools necessary to change your way of looking at things. You're now ready to learn how to use this information to change the way you process information that comes into your brain.

It is not the triggering event itself that produces the anger; it is what goes through the person's mind when prompted by the trigger. Our emotions result from our perceptions, and our perceptions result from our observations plus our preconditioning. Our preconditioning includes our belief system, the way we are trained to respond, and what already exists in that particular memory file. Understanding what this process is and how it works helps us to be able to make changes.

We can train ourselves to respond to potential anger-inducing events in a different way by learning to replace our old habit patterns with new patterns, and by learning to process information differently. Once we choose to respond in a different way, it is a matter of updating our operating systems with the new material so we will get new results when we receive information into our brain.

In a computer, we have to put in the new information and delete the old. We do the same with our brain, but it is much more difficult to delete the old unwanted information. The more you practice this process, however, the more adept you will become.

SEND YOUR NEGATIVE THOUGHTS TO THE THINKING CENTER RATHER THAN THE FEELING CENTER

If life were only to toss us warm fuzzys, it would be easy to feel good all the time. Since life tosses us its normal mix of stuff, we have to learn to make things into warm fuzzys. Every circumstance offers more than one way of looking at it. If you look for the warm fuzzy in each event, you will find it. To do this, you need to change the way you process information in your brain.

One of the keys to eradicating anger is to create a pattern of sending your negative charges to the thinking center instead of the feeling center. For example, you can program, "I am a problem solver and I welcome the opportunity to solve a problem. I love solving problems and coming up with answers." With this new program in place in your memory files, you can learn to process information through your thinking center before you respond, rather than acting out your anger. Even if you still have a negative charge and are still feeling the emotion, you can learn to respond in this way so that your emotions are not intensified. Learning to feel positively about your ability to solve problems will release much of the negative charge from any situation where you previously would have reacted with anger. If you practice this strategy, you will learn to come up with the most *effective* response, rather than the one that you feel like acting out at the moment.

If you're having difficulty figuring out how to program the new message to your brain's memory files, and you're faced with an event that is about to trigger your anger, begin the process by asking yourself, "How important is this anyway?" Having this perspective on an issue will often remove, or at least reduce, the anger. When we respond from our emotions, we tend to dramatize, and things then seem more important to us at that moment than they really are. Asking this question allows you to step back and have a more detached view.

Always give yourself time to think before you respond. You can decide to delay making any decisions when you are experiencing negative feelings. In fact, you can create a new habit of delaying your response. Learn to count to ten. Or "sleep on it" when you're having a hard time finding just the right response to a potential anger-producing situation. Make sure the response seems right to you. Develop a technique that will allow you time to think before you respond. Once you learn to program the right message in your memory files before you respond, you will be able to control your behavior.

Even if you are responding with the desired behavior, any time you feel a cold prickly it's a sign that you still have a problem that needs to be dealt with. If you still experience a negative feeling, go back to the file (memory) where this feeling has its origin and remove the negative charge on that file. Keep working until you no longer experience a negative feeling whenever you open the file (We will explore this in more detail in the next chapter).

When you are able to process negatively charged information through your thinking center before responding, you will set off a positive chain reaction that goes something like this: You'll choose a more effective, positive un-angry behavior. Your changed, positive behavior will in turn have a positive affect on other people, which will cause them to respond more favorably to you. Their positive treatment of you will change your emotional charge to a positive one, because you will not feel as threatened. In this way, the entire chain of emotional and behavioral events will become positively charged!

▲

EXERCISE
Changing the Process

Think about something that makes you respond with anger. For example, maybe your children are habitually late for breakfast. Find a solution to this situation that you are comfortable with and that doesn't leave you with a negative feeling. The next time this situation occurs, use the new solution. If it doesn't work the first time, don't give up. Modify your response or find a better way to present it. If that still doesn't work, then keep trying until you find one that does.

TOOL
Delay Response

Give yourself time to think before you respond. Decide never to make an immediate response when you feel a negative emotion. If it must be dealt with immediately, count to ten before you respond. If you can leave it until later, make a date to deal with it later.

AFFIRMATION
"I do not respond from anger."

▼

CHAPTER 21

Changing The Charges On Your Memory Files

O nce we're aware of how to change the way we process incoming information, we can deal with changing the information that is already in our files (our memories). The information that is already in our files is what gives us an emotional charge when new information is received. By changing the information in our files in a way that reduces or eliminates the negative emotional charge, we can change how we respond to new information when it is received.

In dealing with the positive and negative charges on our files, we want to remove or diminish negative charges and develop as many positive charges as possible. The goal is to remove all negative charges and just have warm fuzzys and neutral charges left in our files. What we are doing is removing or reducing our old angers and bad memories.

In the last chapter, we talked about using the idea of being a problem solver to send the processing of information to the thinking center. This same concept can also be used to reduce the existing negative charges on your files. Here's how this process works. You open your negatively charged, anger-related files. You then program in the idea that you are a problem solver and want to solve problems. After you have changed your beliefs about yourself, when a message comes into that file, it will no longer have that same negative charge. You will then send the information straight to the thinking center for processing, just as you always have for messages without negative charges.

We can apply our new belief system and way of looking at things directly to the information in each file. We use the new beliefs to accept and reprogram what happened in the past either as no longer negative or as totally forgiven. We will then have a new feeling about this old memory when we next revisit it.

If you reach the point where you have been able to open all of your anger-related files and re-program them so that they no longer contain negative charges, you will no longer feel anger. You will have changed your thinking and your life, because you no will longer think and act the same.

You may come across files on which it is extremely difficult for you to change the charges. You may have to keep working on removing the negative charges over and over again. Each time you still feel the anger when an issue relating to that file comes up, do the work again. You may also find additional files that have been hidden away for a long time, which you'll now need to work on to eradicate the negative charge. For example, perhaps you'll unearth a hidden file containing the memory of an old acquaintance from high school that you are still angry with because he or she shamed you in some way. Perhaps this shame is still affecting how you feel about yourself, or people in general, and is therefore also affecting the charges on other files. As new things keep coming up, you will find that you have to go back into areas where you have already made changes in your file charges and make additional changes.

You will also find that in some cases you will have to repeat the process several times before you can access a memory and no longer feel a negative charge. In some cases you may think the negative charge is gone, and then you find it coming back later. This is normal. Do not be too concerned. Just keep making changes wherever and whenever you find cold pricklys.

What is already in our mind when prompted by the anger "trigger" is what is at the root of our anger. By reprogramming our memories so that they are no longer negative, we are using our new belief system and our new way of perceiving to review our past and to change how we feel about it. As we engage in this process, we find that the "anger trigger" no longer has the same effect. Without the negative charge on our memory files, we will no longer employ the beliefs and perceptions that created our anger in the first place.

Now that you know how to evaluate and process incoming information, you can open your existing files and change the charge attached to them from negative to positive, to match your new belief system. As you engage in this practice, you'll find that removing negative charges from old and new files can be the key to an anger-free existence.

▲

EXERCISE

Examining a Negatively Charged File—and Changing it to a Positively Charged File

- Open the file in your mind that contains: "How I feel when someone breaks a promise to me." What kind of a charge do you have on this file? Typically, it will be a negative charge.

- Figure out why you feel negatively and come up with ways to change your thinking so that you no longer attach a negative charge to this particular file. For example, if waiting for a friend who is always late is one of the instances when you must learn to deal in a non-angry way with "someone who breaks a promise," come up with options. Decide to either go without your friend or wait for them. If you choose to wait for them, prepare yourself for their being late by bringing along a book or people-watching. Remind yourself that you have made this choice, fully aware that your friend will likely be late. If you get angry, you need to realize that you are responsible for your anger because you made the choice to wait for a friend whom you know is always late.

EXERCISE
Identifying Negatively Charged Files

Take the time to identify past experiences that have cold pricklys (files with negative charges) attached to them. Review each of these areas of your life:

- Work

- Home

- Health

- Government

- Relationships

- Family of origin

- Friends

- Activities

- **Anything else you can think of that disturbs you in any way.**

Write down the negatively charged files in each of these areas. Come up with as many as possible. Do this on several different occasions to see if you can think of new items to add to the list.

EXERCISE

Changing File Charges

Take each item that you have listed in the exercise above. Open that file in your mind and examine it. Determine what belief(s) you have that makes this file a cold prickly. Consider what beliefs can be changed to remove the negative charge from this file. What way of looking at things (filters) will help you to remove the negative charges, i.e. humor, acceptance, or a new belief. If you are unable to remove the negative charge with a simple review, then apply the Forgiving Old Anger process. If that doesn't work, then review and evaluate.

Set up a program to put a positive charge in place of the negative charge on this file. Do this with all of your files that still have negative charges attached to them. You'll need to prioritize because you will be unable to change more than a few files at the same time. Just keep working. You will be able to find plenty to do.

TOOL

Traffic Scan

If you are stuck in traffic, use the time to scan your feelings. Become aware of what you are feeling in the moment. If you identify a new cold prickly, a new anger that you have not been aware of, jot it down as soon as you get the opportunity. When you have the time, write down the particular anger and the people associated with it. Examine this negatively charged file to determine why you feel the way you do. If you find waiting in traffic a particularly anger-inducing event, use this "traffic scan" exercise as a new behavior pattern that transforms waiting into a positive experience.

▼

CHAPTER 22

Making The Choice To Not Have Anger

What is heaven like? It is a constant state of bliss. When we don't feel anger, we are in such a state of bliss, a state we can fully enjoy when we totally give up our anger. It is within the power of each of us to live a life of warm fuzzys and no longer experience the cold pricklys.

Not having anger is such a freeing feeling. You never have to go to bed at night trying to figure out how to get even. You no longer have to judge how other people are acting. You just accept the world as it is presented to you. You spend your time thinking about the best way to make it work for you. You are able to focus on making decisions that allow you to fully enjoy life. And you do fully enjoy life.

If you value happiness, if you value joy, then make the choice to not allow anger into your life. Just knowing that a life free of anger is available to you once you make the choice to enjoy it, will make you feel better immediately.

Choose to take control of your own life. Don't leave it in the hands of anyone who happens to annoy you. A grudge is a heavy load for anyone to carry, and life is so much lighter without it. Although cold pricklys will be offered to you at every turn, you always have the option of refusing to accept them. And when you realize that it is your own thinking that has to change, not other people's behavior, you are making the choice to take control of your anger and your life.

The management of our emotions is subject to the laws of learning, as in everything else we do. Once we learn a more desirable way to deal with our emotions—so that anger is deflected by supplanting it with a positive thought or idea—we are motivated to make the change. Once we learn how to make the change, it is just a matter of doing the work.

We can learn to embrace fully our positive emotions and, at the same time, reduce and even eliminate our negative ones by changing our belief system and by changing the way we process the messages that come into our brain.

We have explored earlier in the book how you can change your belief system to incorporate beliefs that do not produce anger and expel those that do. Change the way you look at things so that you expect, and only accept, the best in life. Change the way you process things in your brain so that you are responding with your intellect and not just with your emotions. Change your response patterns to positive effective responses. Change your memories by removing all of the old anger feelings from them. Sounds like a tall order. It is, but it can be done if you want to. Learn what needs to be done. Put forth the effort needed to change, and you can become free of the cold pricklys that are now interfering with your full enjoyment of life.

Again, it's what you think, not what happens to you, that counts. Challenge your beliefs that lead to cold pricklys. Get rid of, or change, any belief that is not working for you in the way that you want it to. If we change the "musts" in our lives into preferences, we will reduce many of the negative charges on our files. This will make it much easier to send the input to our thinking center for processing, rather than to the feeling center for action.

WHY WAIT ANY LONGER TO CHOOSE AN ANGER-FREE LIFE?

Many elderly people come to the realization that anger is not worth the toll it takes. They have had enough time to eventually learn the lessons, on their own, from the school of life. With these lessons in mind, they become successful at letting go of their anger. But we don't have to wait until we're older to enjoy a life that's free of anger. We can learn to do it now, before we waste one more day holding onto grudges, judgments, and bad feelings.

To let go of anger, we have to rearrange our thinking so that we choose the belief system of love over the belief system of personal ego. Creating loving relationships is in our own interest as well as the interests of those with whom we come into contact. They will respond positively to our loving nature because that is what they seek in their own lives.

If we can learn to forgive, then we open our hearts and our lives. Remember you are the one who receives the primary benefit of your forgiving. The benefit to the other person is a nice side effect that may pay great dividends to you as well.

We create our own anger, and therefore we can eliminate it. We can learn how to change our thoughts, feelings, and actions and thereby reduce our emotional distress. The time to be joyful and happy is always now. Don't put it off until later. Examine the things that you believe make you unhappy.

Be willing to change your belief system by affirming, "I want a new belief system—I want to believe in the power of smiles, hugs, a kind word, truth, and peace. I want to believe in dreams, imagination, mankind, and having fun."

We can choose a peaceful mind as our only goal in all relationships. We can train our minds to choose peaceful thoughts. Peace is inevitable for those who offer peace. Once we have experienced how pleasant it is to live in a positive state of mind, hanging onto negative thoughts becomes less and less attractive. As we learn to stop upsetting ourselves with our own thoughts, the rewards we will receive will make the work it takes to change seem insignificant.

We have the free will to choose the thoughts we put into our mind. Just as we are not bound by our society's rules to think as others do, we are not bound to think as we used to think. Unchain yourself from the past. Choose to have no anger. Choose happiness.

Top Ten Benefits of not having Anger:

1. We feel good.

2. We like ourselves.

3. We like other people.

4. Other people like us.

5. We experience much less conflict.

6. We have more capacity to love.

7. We function more effectively.

8. We are healthier and tend to live longer.

9. We get more out of life.

10. We are happier.

Start enjoying these benefits! Choose not to have anger by developing your own program for change and working with it. Do it on your own or work with others by attending workshops, discussions, or support groups. You will begin to feel better just knowing there is a more effective way of dealing with your anger. If you are interested in the workshops and seminars that are available through the author, consult the program information contained at the back of this book.

▲

EXERCISE
Cost Benefits Analysis

• List the good things anger does for you.

• List the problems anger causes you.

• Think about them.

• Decide whether you would like to keep your anger or get rid of it.

▼

CHAPTER 23

Making The Commitment

Once you make the decision that you want to remove anger from your life—whether it is over a specific issue or represents a more general anger-filled outlook—your resolve is an important first step. However, your decision will be ineffective unless you do more. It is like making a New Year's resolution. Unless you follow through on your decision to change, your chances of successfully bringing about that change are slim.

My personal plan for removing anger from my life involved the following. I first decided that I no longer wanted to experience anger under any circumstance. Then I decided that any time I felt anger, it was a response that I would refuse to accept as appropriate. No if's, and's, or but's – it would be my mistake to have an angry response to anything, and it was my mission to correct it. I never wasted time with trying to place the blame for my anger on someone or something else.

Once I had made this decision, the rest of the commitment fell into place.

The Anger Response Process:

- Get over it

- Examine what happened to make me angry

- Determine what I need to do in order to not respond with anger the next time

- Do what I need to do to make the change from an angry response to a non-angry response

- Keep practicing until the change is complete

- Appreciate myself every time I make the change to a non-angry response

Every single time I experience anger, I must put myself through this process. Remember that I am not just talking about stuffing the anger. I am talking about actually learning to be free of the feeling. There is a critical difference.

Change requires:

- Understanding where you are

- Knowing where you want to go

- Learning what you have to do to get there

- Setting out on the journey

- Continuing regardless of any setbacks, until you have arrived

THE JOURNEY TO AN ANGER-FREE LIFE

Following through on your commitment to an anger-free life involves signing up for a new journey. Deciding to actually enjoy this journey will make it much more pleasant. Learn to think of life as a process instead of in terms of goals that you are trying to achieve. If you focus only on goals, you are not going to be happy until you have achieved them. If you focus on the process, you will enjoy working to achieve the goals. Since we spend so much of our lives working to achieve goals, doesn't it make sense to enjoy ourselves in the process?

Initially, learning to not experience anger may seem like a lot of work. As you keep working to bring about the change, however, it will become much easier and you will find that your anger flares up much less frequently. One day you will say to yourself, "Gee I can't remember when the last time was that I felt angry."

Your commitment to eradicate anger from your life must include:

- An understanding of how valuable your goal really is

- The passion and desire to achieve it

If you work at it, you will get there. If you do the work and don't lose focus somewhere along the way, you will reach your goal. Refuse to be discouraged by your initial lapses into anger. Instead, learn from those mistakes. Realize that, regardless of the twists and turns along your journey, you are progressing toward your goal—and that you will arrive at "no anger" if you can keep your commitment in place.

Remember to evaluate your progress in reaching the goal of "no anger," but focus more intensely on your successes than on your failures. Encourage yourself. Acknowledge and appreciate the results.

In order to be successful, you need to have unconditional acceptance of both yourself and your goals. Conditional acceptance does not work. You must accept your failures as well as your successes. If you can't accept your failures, then you will ultimately fail, because you will make mistakes in both learning and doing. Keep reminding yourself that you are a better person for committing to and undertaking this important change in your life. You are good, you are worthy, and you are okay. Convince yourself of this with feeling. How you view yourself is your choice. To grow you must accept and love yourself, both as you want to be and as you are.

When you fail, you must intensify your commitment and begin again—and when you do this, you'll find that you will relapse less often. You may discover that you'll need to go through this process again and again—and that's okay. Even if you have many angry outbursts in a week, or even in a day, your renewed commitment to change your angry responses to non-angry ones means you are still doing great. Remember, no matter what conditions exist in your life, you do not have to be angry.

You have the ability to no longer feel anger as long as you maintain your commitment and devise a plan. Set it in motion and keep working at it regardless of setbacks.

Gaining and maintaining the commitment requires thought, feeling, and behavior change—none of which is easy. So give yourself credit and keep telling yourself how much harder your life will be if you don't change. The benefits are worth all that work, many times over. Be willing to do the work, knowing that peace and joy lie ahead.

You can't change, unless you think you can. You must get over, "I tried but I failed therefore I can't." You must realize that you can change your beliefs. Realize you have accomplished difficult things before. Know that change requires significant thought and effort. Stop thinking "I will change;" instead, think, "I am in the process of changing." If you think in terms of changing to an anger-free life as something you will do, you'll be tempted to put off doing the work required to arrive at that new life.

You may find it more effective to commit to changing only one or two of your habitual angry responses at a time. Work with each of them, until you have them pretty well mastered, and then commit to additional changes. If you focus on fewer changes, it will be easier to keep your focus; whereas if you try to change every single instance when an angry response might flair, you might be taking on more than you can find the energy to maintain.

Change comes gradually for most of us. We definitely can change our behavior over time, when we make a commitment to the change. But we need to be realistic with ourselves and realize that transformation doesn't happen overnight. Find a way to focus on your goal. You might write it down and paste it on your mirror or refrigerator. If you have a computer, you can set it up as a screen saver to give you a constant reminder. Or you could share your goals with a friend and use him or her as a frequent "check-in station" to review how you're doing and get input on your problem areas.

In order to give up old habits—whether it's smoking or responding angrily to difficult situations—you need to put as much power into getting rid of them as you did into acquiring them. (Anyone who has ever been a smoker certainly recalls how difficult it was to become a smoker— coughing and suffering through those first cigarettes!) To do something that's challenging, you must have the intention and then commit the power needed for the change. Know that if you had enough power to create the habit, then you have enough power to change it. And don't be discouraged by how long you have had the habit of anger. The power to change is not a function of time—but it does lie within you, waiting to be tapped.

Reasons People Fail When They Try to Change

- They don't commit themselves fully.

- They don't learn what they need to do.

- They don't clearly define their goals.

- They don't allow enough time.

- They don't persevere.

- They don't learn to deal with complexity.

- They don't maintain effort until change is total.

- They don't recognize and reward themselves for small changes.

- They don't recognize their progress.

Accept the Challenge to Remove Anger from Your Life

- Make the choice.

- Commit to doing the work.

- Make the commitment to carry it through.

- Learn what to do.

- Act on your choice.

- Keep acting on it.

- Accept each error with grace.

- Re-evaluate at each error.

- Re-dedicate at each error.

- Keep working toward your goal.

CHAPTER 24

———

Making The Plan

Now you have reached the point where you have decided to get rid of the anger in your life—or at least some specific anger that is particularly upsetting to you. Once you have made the commitment, you must develop a plan so that you can successfully make this change.

MAKING A PLAN TO RID YOURSELF OF ANGER: 6 ESSENTIAL STEPS

1. Decide that you want to respond to everything in your life—or at least some specific things—without anger.

2. Develop a clear statement of your decision so that it is clear exactly what it means to you.

3. Consider what changes must be made in your belief system, in order for you to follow through with your commitment. Determine which old beliefs you must give up and which new beliefs you need to acquire.

4. Determine what new response patterns you will need to develop, as alternatives to anger.

5. Determine what you need to do to acquire these new response patterns.

6. Dedicate yourself to implementing the plan.

Some Important Points to Consider While You Develop Your Plan

- Analyze important problems that trigger your anger

- Avoid tackling too many anger-triggering problems at once

- Set realistic goals and avoid "deadlines"

- Assume that you can find an effective alternative to anger

- Evaluate the pros and cons of an anger-based versus love-based response

- Try several possible love-based responses, to see which works best

- Find out how others have made the desired change/s successfully

Remember that you don't always have to come up with the perfect plan or the ideal alternative to an anger-based response. You just need to find one that you will work for you. Unless you choose a new behavior that is desirable to you, you will never be able to undertake it and use it to replace your old, angry behavior. So choose a behavior that fits your personality, rather than one which you think might make someone else like you better.

Once you create your plan for ridding yourself of anger, judge yourself only on your progress toward your goals. The relevant questions are, "How far do I have left to go?" and "What work do I need to do to get there?" Rate your behavior as "good" when it helps you achieve your goals and as "unacceptable" when it does not. Accept your anger-based responses as an opportunity to learn what not to do next time. In this way, they will become another step toward your goal, rather than a sign of failure.

The most important thing to remember is to never lose focus on what you want to accomplish. Remain committed to your goal of eradicating anger and stick to your plan—or alter it if it isn't working for you. Devise a way to check yourself regularly to see if you are still focused on erasing anger from your life. Initially, you might benefit from a daily "no-anger progress check."

For me, every cold prickly I feel is a reminder that I still have work to do. Learn to pay attention to and never neglect your feelings.

Once you have created your personal plan for how you're going to replace anger with love-based responses, you're ready to implement that plan—which is the subject of the following chapter.

Guidelines for Sticking to Your Plan

- Create your plan

- Resolve to stay focused on your plan

- Determine to act on your decisions

- Acquire knowledge about how to follow through with your plan

- Start acting on that knowledge
- Be steady and persistent
- Accept your failures graciously
- If you fall back on your plan, re-dedicate yourself

▲

EXERCISE
Learning From A Role Model

- As you create your plan for how you're going to rid yourself of anger, write out the answers to the following questions on a sheet of paper:

- Who do I know who models my desired anger-free behavior?

- Why does he/she act that way?

- Why do I respond the way I do?

- What makes it hard for me to change to anger-free behavior?

- What will I need to do to change my way of thinking?

- What will I need to do to change my way of responding?

TOOL
Role Model

A role model can be particularly helpful as you create your plan for eradicating anger. Talk with someone who displays the kind of non-anger behavior you would like to have as part of your plan. Discuss their exemplary behavior with them. Ask them how they came to behave and feel as they do, and how it is helpful for them to be this way. What rewards come to them as the result of being this way? Talk to them also about why you might find it difficult to behave in this way, and ask them what their advice might be.

▼

CHAPTER 25

—

Implementing The Plan

Implementing your plan to remove anger from your life involves practicing new responses, breaking old habits, and creating new ones. Whenever we receive information into our files, in an instant, we process that information, choose a response, and then act. We have relatively little control over the information that comes in. We do, however, have complete control over the action that we choose to take. In order to choose a different response than the one we've habitually chosen in the past, we must change the process in such a way that we will make a different choice the next time we receive the same type of information. In other words, the options we can choose in order to shift from an anger-based to a love-based response system involve changing the way incoming information is processed. This means that in order to change, we do not focus on the problem itself or on our response. Instead, we must focus on how we internally process the problem.

Once we habituate behavior, we find that it is difficult to change. Once we create or accept responses based on our negative emotions, we often hold onto them and have difficulty giving them up. Once our behavior becomes habitual, avoiding it becomes a challenge—even when we know it's the right thing to do. Acting in the way we always have will obviously feel "natural" to us. But when we commit to and make a plan for changing that behavior, so that a new anger-free means of responding can take its place, that new behavior will become "natural" at some point.

With hard work and practice, we can change our behavior. Forcefully, vigorously, and powerfully work at creating better thinking, healthier feelings, and more productive actions. Do this now, not later. For most people, it won't take very long to no longer feel angry about many things. But keep working at changing for the rest of your life if need be. If you keep working on change, you will always continue to improve, even if you never become absolutely perfect at responding in the desired way. And remember that increasing the effort you put into changing will shorten the time it takes you to do so.

The keys to implementing your plan for creating an anger-free life? Having a sufficient desire to make the change and having enough understanding of your own behavior and the process required to change it to draw up an effective plan. Once these are in place, set your plan in motion and keep working on it, regardless of the setbacks. As we discussed earlier, in order to give up a habit, you may need to put the same amount of power behind getting rid of it that you used in acquiring it. If you really focus, you can put a lot of power behind your efforts to change, and accomplish a great deal in a very short period of time.

REHEARSE ANGER-FREE BEHAVIOR

Rehearsing a desired behavior is almost as good as exhibiting the real thing. By repeating an action again and again, you create a new path in your brain until the new response becomes habitual. In this sense, the brain doesn't know the difference between "real" and "rehearsed" behavior. The process is similar to that of memorizing a poem or improving your golf swing. The more times you practice (or rehearse) the poem, the swing, or the anger-free response, the closer you get to that behavior becoming automatic.

You might find it valuable to act out your non-anger response with another person, who takes on the role of your "coach." We know the value of having a coach in sports; likewise, having someone who tells you when you're on track with your new non-angry behavior, and when you're not, is tremendously helpful. For example, you could practice with a friend what your next response will be with a boss who always triggers your anger, a child who tends to push your buttons, or a neighbor who refuses to be a good neighbor. Have your "coach" take the part of the "anger-triggering" person and rehearse with them how you plan to respond the next time.

When you rehearse in this way, you will be imprinting the desired behavior in your mind. By acting it out, rather than just thinking about a desired behavior, you will be well on your way to implementing your plan.

Why did it take me so long to break my habit of looking in wrong cupboard for the cereal bowl when my wife moved it to another cupboard that I referred to earlier? I never took the time to set up a new mental picture and never rehearsed the new response. I just did not feel it was worth the effort to work on the problem. The habit seemed too unimportant to expend any time and effort on. I kept forcing myself to correct to the right response until it became the new habit—but I ended up spending a lot more time than I needed to in making the change because I didn't put the effort into mindfully practicing the desired new behavior.

ASSESSING YOUR PROGRESS

How do you maintain your improvement? An important part of implementing your plan is figuring out what to do when you lapse back into your old habit of responding with anger. When you fall back, try to pinpoint what you changed to bring about your original improvement. Keep thinking and rethinking. Keep discovering and disputing related anger issues. Assess your progress. Decide how to continue. Observe how you are doing. Plan new possible moves. Push yourself. Reflect on how you are doing. If you need to, revise your plan and continue.

If this doesn't work for you, and you find the problem is more complex, try thinking of yourself as a problem solver who enjoys solving problems. Enjoy the challenge of finding a solution that works. If this still doesn't work, then the problem may be more complicated. Go back and change the charge you have on that file. Look for beliefs that you need to change. You may even end up finding old anger that needs to be released. Continue to be your own "anger detective" until you figure out what part of the process you need to work on to solve the problem.

Always review events that make you feel angry or irritable, or that elicit complaints or criticisms. Write down what happened and how you felt. Reviewing what took place and expressing it in a written form will help you form a judgment about how you should best view the event. Always look for any way you can change your thinking so that you will no longer feel anger in this situation. In reviewing your behavior, replay the situation the way you would like it to be. Regard undesirable results as water under the bridge. Accept your backsliding. Figure out why it happened. Determine how you can behave differently the next time. Re-dedicate yourself to doing whatever it takes to rid yourself of anger.

Don't forget to review events where your response was positive and not based in anger. Acknowledge your progress and give yourself credit! If you are happy with your response, this will reinforce it. Think about applying this response to other situations as well, in order to build on your success. Congratulate yourself for responses you are satisfied with—even when you might be tempted to consider them "no big deal." Even small triumphs over anger help create bigger ones. So always take a moment to appreciate your successes.

As with negative responses, it is also helpful to write down those instances when you successfully triumphed over anger. Keeping track in this way helps you appreciate your progress. Consider keeping a diary on each individual problem that you are dealing with so that you can better understand and track your progress.

As you put your best effort into implementing your plan to erase the anger from your life, give yourself a reward for right action and accept failures. Do something nice for yourself. Treat yourself to a pleasant lunch once a week. Keep yourself in a good mood. Find something to laugh at every day.

Principles to Keep in Mind When Making Changes in Your Life

- Permanent change takes time.

- Perseverance always pays off.

- Success builds on itself.

Guidelines for Making Changes in Your Life

- Be determined to act on your commitment to change.

- Acquire the necessary knowledge to implement your plan to change.

- If one plan doesn't work effectively, devise a new one and move on with your efforts to change.

- Rehearse the desired change until it becomes habitual.

- When you have a relapse into undesired behavior: accept yourself fully, re-commit to change, acquire more knowledge, assess what went wrong, take action to bring change, keep persisting in your efforts.

- Do not consider relapse as failure.

- Give yourself encouragement.

- Celebrate your victories—large and small.

▲

TOOL

Keep A Diary of How Your Anger-Free Plan IS Working

A written record of your "anger/non-anger response" successes and relapses will help you identify what you're doing right and what you still need to work on. As soon as possible after an anger-inducing or potential anger-inducing event occurs...

- Record what happened when you responded to a potential anger-inducing situation in an un-angry way.

- Record what happened when you "relapsed" by responding with anger to a particular situation.

- Use these guidelines to help you record what happened:

  - What upset you?

  - Describe what an impartial observer would have seen or heard. (Don't Include your own thoughts or actions)

  - What thought went through your mind just before you responded to the event?

  - What did you do or say in response to the event?

  - If you responded without anger, what technique did you use?

- If you responded with anger, what anger-free response might you use next time a similar situation arises?

- What is holding you back from applying the anger-free response?

- What do you need to change so that you will be able to apply the anger-free response?

TOOL
"Rehearsing" Anger-Free Behavior

Explain to a friend the new behavior you want to practice. Have the friend attempt to trigger your anger by acting out the behavior that upsets you. Respond with the new non-angry response that you desire. Rehearse this new behavior until you no longer have any negative feelings about this issue.

CHAPTER 26

Dealing With Other People's Anger

Most often the anger directed at us is due to the other person having different expectations than ours. They are operating under the assumption that we will act toward them in a certain way; but when we don't, their anger is triggered. They may hold very different beliefs, be totally unaware of our point of view or motivation, or they simply may be very different from us in many ways. In dealing with another person's anger, it's important to be aware of the fact that the other person wants something to come out of their relationship with you. The key is to understand their expectations, and to help them understand yours.

Such mutual understanding is brought about by meaningful communication. Rather than expecting the other person to feel the same way as you do about the situation that's made them angry, make a real effort to find out how they really feel. In order to get a real understanding of what's driving their anger—so that you can ultimately diffuse it—you'll need to hone your listening and communication skills.

HOW LISTENING AND COMMUNICATING CAN DIFFUSE ANGER

Train yourself to be a good listener by learning how to "listen deeply." To do this, you must put your own thoughts and beliefs aside, and really focus on what the other person is saying.

Unfortunately, most conversations can be characterized as "my stuff/your stuff." They can be likened to a strange "game" of tennis—played with two separate balls. You serve your ball to me. I let it pass and serve my ball back to you. You let it pass and serve your ball back to me. The game continues in this way—with neither player receiving the other person's ball. In such an instance, it obviously isn't a game at all. And in a conversation with the same characteristics, it's not really a conversation at all. You want to tell your story and I want to tell mine. We never hear the other person's story because we are too busy telling our own. How many conversations have you had lately that went this way?

We can diffuse another person's anger simply by putting an end to the "my stuff/your stuff" game and truly listening to that person. Interestingly, very often when you give an angry person the courtesy of politely listening to what they have to say, without interrupting them or retaliating in anger, their anger is reduced.

As you're listening, focus on the feelings being expressed by the other person, rather than the strict meaning of their words. The feelings are the most important part of any message. When a child tells us, "Billie hit me," we tend to focus on the hit instead of how the child feels. If you can respond in a way that lets the child know you understand how he feels, this will tend to calm him down. For example, "It sounds like you feel hurt and angry." Learn to deal with an angry person's feelings in this way. Their feelings are usually far more important than the event itself.

Most people find it very difficult to directly express their feelings. When someone hurls an angry remark at you, learn to put yourself in his or her shoes. Becoming aware of what the other person is experiencing emotionally requires that you set your own feelings aside. Look to see if you have triggered their anger in any way. Look to see how you might be causing the disturbed feelings.

Are there particular methods of communicating with someone that will diffuse their anger? Try this: Summarize what you think the angry person has said, without injecting anger into your statement. Repeat both the ideas and the feelings that you believe they have expressed. Hearing their own sentiments expressed back to them in a calm way tends to pacify an angry person. Getting their passion acknowledged and their needs met diffuses their anger and helps them to move from their own emotional center into their thinking center. You may need to repeat your "calmed down version" of what you think they were trying to express, but if you can learn to be patient with an angry person and employ this method, you will validate them and eliminate their anger.

Open up to the person who is angry with you. Establish a bridge. Communicate kindness and this will likely change the way they relate to you. It will be difficult for them to maintain their anger at someone who is being pleasant and kind.

When you communicate with someone who may be holding onto a lot of anger, the best way to deal with him or her is to show a genuine interest in them as a person and in the way that they view life. You'll likely find that when you communicate in this way, their defenses will drop and their hearts will open. Your authentic concern for them is a powerful diffuser of anger.

FEELING COMPASSION FOR THE ANGRY PERSON

Most people naturally love and want love returned. It is part of our nature to love others. Ask yourself these questions: How can I react toward others to prevent pushing their anger buttons? How should I react toward others to avoid having their anger push my anger buttons? Once you have identified these "hot buttons" you can adjust your behavior so that it will not incite or intensify the anger of others.

If you feel compassion, then another person's anger will no longer cause you to become angry. Compassion is possible only when you have an understanding of what that person might be going through. Once you learn to be more aware and caring about the other person's feelings, you will start developing responses that are not anger producing.

You can choose to see everyone as either loving or fearful. We offer help to the fearful, not anger. For example: You are remodeling your office. A consultant is brought in to supervise the work. He is rude and abrasive. Do you feel angry with him? Suppose you knew he was suffering from a deteriorating illness? Be aware that the other person's anger is usually not incited by something you said to him. It usually originates from some underlying problem that he has in his life that has nothing to do with you. Learn to see that the angry person is the cause of his own anger, and that the fault does not lie with you.

Anger is a message that can be read as a cry for help: "Pay attention to me. I don't like what you are doing. Restore my pride. Give me justice. You are in my way. I am afraid." Think of a person who is angry as a person who is in need of help.

To most of us, anger seems personal. If someone gets angry with us, we feel they deserve retaliation. That kind of thinking only serves to escalate the anger and perpetuates all sorts of problems. This is one of the reasons nations go to war with each other. When you learn to become compassionate and to fully convince yourself that you can withstand the angry jibes other people send your way, you create choices for yourself. You can choose to turn away from the angry person or stay with them and enjoy their positive attributes. You may even enjoy showing them how they can be less angry just by your own example. With compassion as your guide, you will not only be less likely to receive other people's anger, you will be creating a more loving environment.

Respond with love and compassion, rather than punishment and retaliation, and an angry person will be disarmed. Trade the need to be right for a loving relationship. It is a trade you – and everyone around you – will benefit from.

Do you have a friend who...

- believes people are constantly trying to put them down?

- believes they should have things exactly how they want them?

- believes that if people do something wrong, they must be punished?

- believes you take no notice of them unless they act irritated or angry?

- believes people are selfish, self-centered, and unhelpful?

- believes people are hostile and angry?

Life isn't much fun with this belief system. Have compassion for your friend. Model behavior that will encourage friends like this to change their anger-based beliefs. Maintaining a friendship with people whose beliefs consistently lead to anger may be very difficult for you. If they don't show signs of wanting to change, you may find your life happier without them in it.

Principles to Keep in Mind When Dealing With the Anger of Others:

- Other people's anger is usually not about you.

- Only your own thoughts and attitudes can upset you, not the anger of others.

- Other people are worrying about their problems, not yours.

- Forgiving and apologizing eliminate anger.

Guidelines for Dealing with the Anger of Others:

- Listen to what the angry person is saying, and perceive the feeling underneath their words.

- Summarize the angry person's feelings back to them, so that they know you understand what they're going through.

- Understand the angry person's reality, and show them compassion.

- Choose to perceive other people as loving or fearful, not as attacking.

- Acknowledge that forgiving and apologizing eliminate anger.

- Model anger-free behavior.

Be how you want others to be. They will respond in kind. The rewards you receive will be many times worth the effort.

▲

EXERCISE
Listening to the Angry Person

The next time you are the target of someone else's anger, listen to what the angry person is saying. Decipher what the feelings are beneath what they are saying. Express your compassion for their feelings. Notice how this makes them feel.

TOOL
Time-Out

When you find yourself about to respond angrily to the anger of another, tell them you'd like to take a "time out" (i.e., twenty minutes or so) to think things over. Go somewhere where you can relax, or even lie down. Resume your discussion once you've "cooled off"— and see if this doesn't help you to deflect the other person's anger.

TOOL
Who Has the Problem?

When confronted by someone who is directing his or her anger at you, ask yourself, "Who has the problem?" The answer is always, "The person with the anger." Remind yourself that once you realize this, *you* don't have to be upset. This realization will help to calm you down and allow you to stay in your thinking brain. Think, "What can I do to help this person?"

TOOL

Summarize Back

A powerful way to diffuse someone's anger is to objectively summarize back to him or her, in a very calm way, what you think they said to you. Don't add your own interpretations or feelings. Simply summarize *their* ideas and feelings. Use your thinking center to stay centered. This is not easy to do at first, and requires a lot of practice. Say something like, "I understand that you are telling me _____ and that you feel_____ about it."

▼

CHAPTER 27

Dealing With Anger In Relationships

A relationship between partners is intimate and intense—and for this reason anger issues become intensified. More is at stake than with a casual acquaintance or friend. So if we want to maintain the relationship, it becomes even more important for us to remove the anger.

How well we get along with our mate affects our entire quality of life. We spend most of our time with this person, and if we don't know how to deal effectively with the anger that arises between us, we are going to have major problems. In this chapter, we will address some of the special problems inherent in a couple relationship and offer insights that are helpful in dealing with anger.

ACCEPTANCE, RESPECT, AND APPRECIATION

If you are going to move beyond the anger, you must respect your mate and accept them just as they are. You will not be able to enjoy a happy intimate relationship unless you fully *accept* and *respect* the other person, and let them know that you do. "Never criticize or complain" is a good rule to follow. It will help you to reap great rewards in the richness of your relationship.

Never think you have the right to decide for your partner what is right or what they should do. This means you are attempting to assume a position of power over them. If you assume that power, your relationship is no longer an equal one. Also, the other person usually will not accept your control. They will likely become angry and unhappy with the relationship in some way.

Intimacy with your mate requires that you respect and appreciate them for the person that they are. If you do, it will be easier to deepen your friendship and love. If you don't respect your partner, focus on learning to respect them, because it is essential to the relationship.

Focus your attention on the things that make your mate special and that attracted you to them initially. Always, always appreciate that. Often, and with enthusiasm, tell your mate how much you love and appreciate them. Doing this can prevent and dissolve a lot of anger.

BE OPEN ABOUT YOUR EXPECTATIONS

Our expectations can often get in the way of intimacy—especially when we're not forthcoming with our mate or when expectations clash. We need to let our mate know what our expectations are, find out what their expectations are, and then come to some agreement about them. Preferably, we should do this before we enter into any permanent or long-term relationship.

Your mate's expectations will always be different than yours. To assume otherwise will only get you into trouble. Too often, we expect that our relationship will or should resemble how things were in our family or how "most couples" relate to each other in this society. We then become partners with someone expecting that they will think and act that way. But we have no right to expect that our prospective partner live up to our expectations, unless they agree to. Just because they have agreed to enter into a relationship with you does not mean that they have agreed to do the cooking and the cleaning, or anything else that you may consider customary and expect from them. Anything you consider important in your relationship should be agreed to ahead of time by both of you. When new things come up as your relationship progresses, they should be worked out mutually. You have no right to be angry just because your mate doesn't want to do things your way. Their idea of what is expected and what they are willing to contribute are just as important as yours are. Expecting them to conform to your notion of how a partner should be, when they haven't agreed to those expectations, and becoming angry when they don't live up to them, is unfair and unreasonable.

USE THE METHODS YOU'VE LEARNED IN THIS BOOK

When you are angry with your mate, work on it, using the methods we've explored in this book. Ask for their help; take time, disclose, and understand. Say to your partner; "Please help me. I need your help in figuring out how to curb my anger." The other person will want to do their best to help you when you can explain why you got angry. Explain what you are feeling. Explain as best you can what belief is behind the feelings that incited your anger.

Listen to what your mate has to say. Do not play the "You said/ I said" game. Learn to summarize back to them what you think they said. If you listen to them, they will appreciate it. To listen and really hear what the other person says is not a difficult skill to learn if you pay attention. You will both learn from it. It will create intimacy. There will be much less negative emotion resulting from misunderstanding what the other person is saying and feeling. And their feedback regarding your anger will likely help you to choose the right methods to combat it.

BECOME MORE FAMILIAR WITH YOURSELF

The first step to true intimacy is to know and understand, and to become intimate with, your self. Your self is what you bring into the relationship. If you don't know your self, or are ashamed of part of it, you won't be able to fully share your self with your partner. You will hide and protect unhealed wounds. You will not offer your self fully to another, as is required for true intimacy, unless you feel good about the self you are offering.

This means we must make a journey into our own selves to learn about our defense mechanisms, to deal with our fears, and remove our anger. Only then can we reach the core of love that is at the heart of who we are.

UNLEARN ABUSIVENESS

Abusiveness is learned. It is not a personality defect or illness. It is an inappropriate acting out of anger. The feeling is overwhelming at the time, but it can, and must be, unlearned if you are to have a successful relationship.

Abusiveness is a mutual problem because you both have to live with it. One partner may be abusive and the other provides the trigger. It can be helpful to alter the triggering events, but the responsibility lies in changing the abusive behavior. The abused party should never feel responsible for changing his or her behavior in order to prevent the abuse. Abusiveness is an effort to solve a problem in an ineffective and emotional way. Other, more successful ways for solving problems can be learned.

DON'T BECOME MIND READERS

We need to learn to not make assumptions about what our partner is thinking or wants. Also, we should never assume that they fully understand what we are telling them. Finishing your partner's sentence for them when you think you know what they're about to say not only leads to their resentment and anger but to your own lack of understanding about who they really are.

On the other hand, be clear when you're communicating something to your partner. Don't assume that the other person automatically knows what you mean when you say something. Their way of thinking is not identical to yours, and misunderstandings are likely if you are not explicit and clear. Such misunderstandings can often lead to one or the other person becoming angry. We need to do the best we can to make sure the other person understands what we are thinking and that we understand what they are thinking.

OWN UP TO YOUR MISTAKES

Disclose and admit to errors. You will diffuse, or even prevent, a lot of anger if you are quick to own up to your mistakes. A sincere apology, and not repeating the mistake, is a great redeemer. Become aware of your own and your mate's anger triggers and assumptions that lead to anger.

If we are not feeling anger, then we are free to feel love. Free yourself from the anger in your relationship and you will feel the love.

▲

TOOL
Feeling Time

Take some time on a regular basis to sit down with your mate and talk about feelings. Tell them all of the good things they do that make you feel good. Then have them do the same. Next talk about the things that are happening that result in cold pricklys for you and for them. Try to understand why you feel differently. Find ways to remove the cold pricklys. Work on them together.

TOOL
Time-Out

Take a "time-out" (about twenty minutes) when either one of you is upset and requests it. Use the time to think things over, lie down, and relax. Afterwards, you can resume your discussion. This tool is especially helpful when you are both angry. It will help you to get out of your feeling center and back into your thinking center.

TOOL
Working Out Differences

Sit down with your partner and work out a *mutually agreeable plan* to improve a particular problem area, one that typically results in one or the other of you becoming angry.

For example, work out a mutually agreeable plan to share household responsibilities, so that neither of you resents doing more than their fair share. Regardless of the compromises involved, your plan will prevent you from expecting the other person to do chores they haven't committed to and then getting angry when those chores aren't done.

Devise a similar mutually agreeable plan for working out differences in any other area of your relationship.

CHAPTER 28

Parenting Without Anger

Although parenting may be our most challenging relationship, there is never an adequate reason for allowing anger to enter into it. Sadly, many parents respond angrily to their children's behavior, take out their anger on their children, or act out angrily in front of them. Most of us know this is not the right way to respond. However, anger aimed at children remains a serious problem in our society.

How we deal with our problems sets an example for our children. Unfortunately, many parents become the models for anger, unintentionally passing such behavior on to their children. When this is the case, as the child develops he or she tends to respond with anger both internally and behaviorally.

TEACH YOUR CHILD LOVE, NOT ANGER

We use anger in disciplining our children because we become upset by what they do, and we then become angry. We then tend to mix our anger in with the lessons we are trying to teach the child. But when we mix the "lesson" with our anger, we end up teaching our child that it's okay to respond with anger to things that upset us. When we respond with anger, the child learns anger. As parents we often don't even realize that we are using anger. So the first step in dealing with your anger as a parent is to become aware of how you feel when you relate to your children.

When we respond out of love, the child learns love. If we are free of anger, we teach our children love, not anger. We give them a life of warm fuzzys. Just knowing that we can raise our child without anger should be reason enough for us to put forth the effort to get rid of our own anger.

Learn to talk about feelings with your children. Find out what upsets them and why. Find out why they feel the way they do. Work with them to solve their problems and to release their anger. Even though their friends display anger, they can learn from you that they don't need to use it themselves. Teach them that they can be far more effective, and accomplish more as a person, if they are not controlled by anger. Teach them how not to have anger by using some of the methods you have learned about in this book.

Teach your values and rules to your children, but allow them to make decisions for themselves. Teach them to think; don't just tell them what to do. Accept their mistakes as an indication of what lessons they still need to learn. When your children become adults, release them from your control completely. Respect them for who they have become, and tell them so. Your children are obligated to follow the general rules of our society, but they are not obligated to observe them in the exact way you do. They are also not obligated to accept and follow the family rules they grew up with. Respect and accept their choices.

It is our job as parents to teach our children how the world works. They acquire most of their belief system from us. Learn how to deal with anger so you can teach your children how to be free from it as well.

PERMISSIVENESS IS NOT LOVE, AND ASSERTIVENESS IS NOT ANGER

Parenting without anger doesn't mean you don't have to discipline your children. You can, however, discipline them with love instead of anger. Children need to learn boundaries. They must learn the rules of our society. Teach them these things with love. Permissiveness is not love. And assertiveness is not anger. Model love for them, and they will see the value in not being angry. Remember your child needs values, your time, and love, not things. Worthwhile values are imparted when you parent with love. The reward for this style of parenting is a happy and independent child with whom you will have a loving relationship for the rest of your life. Always remember to treat your children with love.

Never accept anger from your child as appropriate behavior. Children learn to use anger when it is effective for them. They will keep using it as long as it works. Part of our job, as a parent is to not allow anger to be effective for our children. It is our job to show them a more effective way to deal with their problems. Whenever your child is angry, lovingly demonstrate to him or her that it is not appropriate behavior. Teach your child to find a more effective way of dealing with problems. As soon as your child is old enough to communicate verbally, teach them about expressing and dealing with their feelings.

Teach your children about warm fuzzys and cold pricklys and how to recognize them. Use these terms as a method for them to let you know how they feel about things as they happen. When you are in doubt about how they feel, ask them if what they're feeling is a warm fuzzy or a cold prickly.

Families often focus on telling their children what to think and do. Learn to talk about the feelings, and always point out the reasons for your rules and decisions, taking into account the child's feelings and the positive side of what you're asking of them. We use "don't" with our children far too often. Always try to find out from your child why they want to do something. Consider their request, and then lovingly explain why it is not possible when it isn't.

Once you have taught your child inappropriate behavior, it can become very difficult to help the child learn a new and appropriate way of responding. When faced with a problem in relating to your child, there are two important rules to keep in mind. First, always respond out of love. Second, when you are unsure of the answer, spend some time and effort learning what you should do.

I know a couple of special children who were raised without being taught to be fearful. They were raised with love. They were not taught to be fearful in disturbing situations. They believed that they could solve any problem. They learned total acceptance—acceptance of themselves and others, and acceptance of the goodness of the world. They learned to trust and love the world. They learned to operate from a positive emotion of love. They learned to respond from their thinking center rather than from their negative emotions. They are problem solvers. They do not feel themselves to be fearful in situations that would call forth the negative emotions of fear and anger in most others. They pretty much see the world as a loving world. They don't fear the world. To have such an outlook on life is the greatest gift a parent can give to their children.

If you raise your child in this way, you will be giving them this gift—and it will reward them richly for the rest of their lives.

▲

TOOL

List Your Child's Angry Responses...and Create a Plan to Get Rid of Them

Make a list of your child's anger responses. If he or she is old enough to understand, find out from them what upsets them. Now make and carry out a plan to remove the cold pricklys from your child's life.

TOOL

Commit to Never Being Angry with Your Child

Make a commitment to yourself to work at never being angry with your children. This commitment is based on the principle that getting angry with a child is never the acceptable response. Any time you find yourself angry with your children, commit yourself to finding the reason and changing your way of responding so that it will not happen again.

Also, make a commitment that you will not display angry behavior in front of your child. If you find you still must act out some anger, commit yourself to doing it where your children can't see you.

TOOL
Time-Out—For YOU As Well As Your Child

When either of you is upset, use a time-out to allow emotions to cool off. This goes for you as well as your child. Especially use time-outs when you are both angry. Use the time-out procedure to get yourself out of your feeling center and back into your thinking center. When you are able to deal with the issue without anger, return to it and deal with it in an appropriate way.

▼

CHAPTER 29

Dealing With Persistent Present Anger

What if, in spite of everything you've tried, you still feel angry? What do you do about it? How do you release the anger so that you're finally rid of it? The bad news is that it may not be easy. But it can be done; if you know how, if you want to do it, and if you do the work.

When we are emotionally distressed, we have negative thoughts, and we often have strong faith in those thoughts. Many of us are very strongly attached to our own way of thinking. We sometimes find it very difficult to accept that there are other ways of looking at things that are okay.

When you feel angry, remember that anger is prompted by fear. Ask yourself what you are afraid of. Ask yourself what you are thinking that makes you feel this way. Look for the hidden reasons behind the feeling.

Take the time to examine how you really feel. Be honest with yourself. Put in the effort to understand your anger. Practice looking deeply within yourself to see the nature of your anger. Take care of your anger the same way that you take care of your physical body. Learn to identify your anger.

How does it feel? Be aware of the physical signs of anger. Notice the changes in your body. Notice your breath, hands, body warmth, and body tension. Be sensitive to your internal signs of anger. Once you recognize them, they can help you identify when you're about to get angry.

When you get angry, acknowledge your anger and decide what to do with it. Recognize and embrace anger when it surfaces, instead of suppressing it. The first step to overcoming your anger is to acknowledge that it is present and that you are committed to dealing with it. Once you own your anger you can control its expression.

Responses You can Choose to Deal with Persistent Anger:

- Send the anger to your thinking center to find the most effective response.

- Keep quiet until you get over it.

- Use self-talk to work it through.

- Set it aside and pick it up later.

- Talk about your feelings to someone.

- Use any distraction, such as music or exercise.

Develop a backup plan to nip anger in the bud when your other anger-free plans aren't working.

Emergency Measures to Nip Anger in the Bud:

- Disengage immediately. Just don't talk anymore about it.

- Use a key word or phrase to tell yourself to get off the anger track. For example: Stop, This is funny, Time to relax, I don't want to feel this way, It's time to change my thinking.
- Use a time-out.

THE DO'S AND DON'TS OF TALKING ABOUT YOUR ANGER

It helps to talk through an emotion, either with yourself or with a friend. You need to be very careful how you do this, however. If you are merely relating how you are feeling and why, you are rehearsing your anger instead of reducing it. When you retell the circumstances that triggered your anger, you become aroused again. This actually reinforces and justifies your anger. You buy into your own story. So, instead of just talking about it, examine the event and your reaction. Discuss why you are feeling angry. Discuss what caused it. Discuss what you can do to get over it.

You can also talk about the upsetting event with the person who upset you. If you do decide to talk about the event, don't talk about how angry you are and what you want to happen. Instead talk about the feelings and beliefs underneath your anger. Try to determine what you think is making you feel this way. Remember that most people don't like to listen to anger. Tell the other person that you are not asking them to fix it for you, but only to listen to you so you can listen to yourself think. Tell them that your talking to them is just so you can better understand the situation. There is no shame in being angry. Everyone has felt this way. There is no reason to hide your feelings as long as you are expressing them in appropriate ways. Express your feelings while they are still fresh. Be clear, and focus on talking about the fear and pain that you feel. Don't fight against the anger. Instead transform it into understanding and compassion.

If you are unable to prevent the expression of your anger, *at least* control how you express it. You can express your anger in ways that allow others to receive it. The expression of strong anger is usually seen by others as an attack.

Shift your expression from aggression to assertion. You can be assertive and get your point across forcefully without being aggressive. Being assertive means firmly and rationally stating your position, and removing any anger from your statement.

State your feelings in a way that shows your sincerity but leaves the other person a choice of accepting or rejecting your position. Maybe you can even add, "and I would love you for doing this." When you are angry, confess it. It is okay to let someone know when you are upset with what they are telling you. Still, you can use loving speech.

Expressing our anger directly pushes the other person away. Awareness of this may help you in letting go of your anger. Say to yourself, "I like that person," " I want them in my life," "I want them to be happy with me."

Admit it to yourself when you are angry. Notice it. Attend to it. Let yourself feel upset a little if need be. Then decide whether or not you want to talk about it with a friend or the person involved. You may decide that talking about it is not the most effective way of dealing with the issue that upset you. If that is the case, there are other methods you can try.

USE LOVING THOUGHTS...AND GIVE UP ON CONTROLLING PEOPLE

Realize that what you are thinking may be hurting you. Choose to replace your negative thoughts with loving positive thoughts. People want to be loved. If you hold back your anger and give them love instead they will respond in a positive way. When others are positive, it is easier for you to be positive. Ask yourself, "If I was feeling love, what would I do now?" Realize that the other person is not intentionally trying to hurt you. They are just doing the best they can. Do not blame other people for not playing by the rules. They are living life by their rules, not yours.

Remember that you have no right to control other people. The fact that they have done something you think is wrong gives you no right to control them or to try to change them. Remind yourself of this when you are upset at how others are acting. Once you tell yourself, "I do not control what other people do," you free yourself from anger.

HUMOR, COMPASSION, AND PLEASANT DISTRACTIONS

You can learn to reframe your anger as humor. Laugh at yourself for feeling the way you do. This can help a lot – especially in minor situations, such as being cut off in traffic or being upset that someone has hindered your plans in some way. Often, just laughing at yourself or the situation, or thinking that what the other person says or does is humorous, will diffuse your anger immediately.

If you find expressing humor difficult, learn to feel compassion for the other person. You can learn to feel sorry that the person who cuts you off in traffic is so rushed or stressed that he has to do that.

If you keep quiet about momentary irritations and distract yourself in pleasant activity until you settle down, chances are you will feel better faster than if you let yourself get into a shouting match. Letting your anger out usually makes it worse. Force yourself to act differently than you may feel like doing. People who haven't developed inhibitions cause social problems. Normally anger doesn't continue to build up inside. Instead it dissipates. Sometimes it doesn't, and we hold on to old angers, a problem we will deal with in the next chapter. But if yours is not an "old anger," use the methods and suggestions in this chapter.

5 Ways to Reduce Persistent Anger

1. **Slow down your adrenaline flow.** Learn to relax. Be mentally flexible. Let go of your musts. Accept the world.

2. **Reduce the amount of stress in your life.** If you are upset by rush-hour traffic, find a way to avoid it. If something needs fixing, and it bothers you, fix it.

3. **Change the beliefs that are causing your anger.** Identify the beliefs that are creating your anger. Question those beliefs, challenge them, and change them.

4. **Process your negative emotions through your thinking center.** Develop the habit of always sending negative emotions to your thinking center before you choose a response.

5. **Remove or reduce the negative charges from your memory files.** Whenever you find a cold prickly, search

your beliefs to find the cause and change to a new belief that does not elicit a cold prickly.

5 Essential Points to Remember in Getting Over Persistent Anger

1. Pounding a pillow or punching bag won't help you get over a nagging anger. You'll only be acting out your anger. The other person is spared, but you are not.

2. There is no set time frame for getting over your anger.

3. It is appropriate to modify your angry behavior, but don't suppress your feelings. If you do, they'll show up in the future as a new problem.

4. Expressing your feelings does not mean acting out your anger. You can learn to express your anger without acting it out.

5. Remember that you feel the way you think. So if you are angry, it means you are going to have to go back and change the way you think. As soon as you are able to move past feeling your anger, the next step is to go back and examine your thinking.

Although there is no set time frame for getting over something that angers you, if you simply can't stop acting out your anger or if it continues to depress you, then it is time to find outside help. Agencies and support groups are available if you do not choose professional counseling. Remember that you are going to have the problem until you fix it.

▲

TOOL
Relaxation

Sit quietly in a comfortable position.

Close your eyes.

Deeply relax all your muscles—from your feet to your head.

Breath through your nose.

Be aware for ten to twenty minutes.

Feel empowered to make the changes you desire.

TOOL
Self-Talk

When you are experiencing anger, talk to yourself about it. Ask yourself, "Why am I angry?" Tell yourself why your feelings aren't right. Remind yourself how you want to think about the situation that's making you upset. Laugh at yourself for feeling the way you do. **Just keep working at it until the feeling has dissipated.**

TOOL
Time-Out

If you're angry about something on your own, or about a discussion you're having with someone else, give yourself a 20-minute time-out.

Use the time to lie down and relax and reconsider the course you are on. Give yourself some time to think through and change your potentially angry response – especially when you are angry with someone who is also angry with you.

TOOL
Reverse Role-Playing

Have a friend play the part of the angry you. Then you take the other side of the issue and try to convince "yourself/your friend" not to have anger. This will help you to reframe the issue in a non-anger inducing way that you can accept. For example, your friend might take your position by saying, "I am upset with Bill because he always goes out to play golf when he is needed at home." You would then try to convince "yourself/your friend" that they shouldn't be upset with Bill.

TOOL
Record and Evaluate

As soon as possible, after each time you get angry, write down what you were angry about, how you felt, and what you did to try to change your feelings.

Soon after you no longer have the negative feelings, review the situation. Ask yourself:

- **What thinking made me feel anger?**

- **What beliefs do I need to change?**

- How can I better view the problem?

- What is an effective, non-anger response I can use?

Practice your new response. When the situation arises again, use your new response.

TOOL
Replacing Anger

Any time you feel anger, or you have chosen the wrong response, review the event and decide how you would have preferred to respond. Practice this new behavior in your mind. Rehearse it and be ready to use it the next time the same or a similar situation arises. If your new behavior doesn't work, forgive yourself and try again.

TOOL
Listen to the Eagles

Get a copy of the song "Get Over It," by the Eagles. Listen to it. Allow yourself to relax and enjoy the message.

▼

CHAPTER 30

Releasing Old Anger

There is a deep-seated kind of anger that we tend to hold onto longer than any other type. Since it is often too painful to deal with, we find a way to suppress it. We may have even forgotten that it's there. Then something happens that makes us unconsciously call up something from our past, and we get angry, upset, and pained. Until we become conscious of these old angers from our past, we can't be free of them.

Sometimes we're aware of how old angers continue to influence us, and sometimes we're not. They are often buried so deeply that the only way we feel them is in the effects they continue to have on us. For example, you may feel angry about something and not be aware that it stems from a painful experience you had early in your life. And yet, that experience continues to influence how you feel and act today.

If we are going to really enjoy this life, we need to bring these old hurts to the surface, review the old files, and remove the negative emotional charge attached to them so that they no longer rule our lives.

FAMILY BAGGAGE

The most common cause of old anger is unresolved issues from our family of origin. Not only are such angers the most common, they are also the strongest and often the most deeply buried. We bury these angers because we don't want to keep feeling the hurt and because we need to be able to function in our family and in the world.

We learn a particular belief system from our families, but as we become adults we change at least part of that system, so that some of our old beliefs no longer fit. Spend some time thinking about your family. Think about the good stuff you learned from them. Appreciate what they did for you. Now take the time to find all of the stuff you got from them that you no longer need, stuff that is holding you back from fully enjoying your life. Write down all of the stuff that hurts when you think about it. Write down all of the stuff that holds you back from being what you want to be. Identify the negative stuff that you are still holding onto and run it through the process to remove the negative charges.

Now is the time to unload your anger—and your family baggage—by resolving those issues that cause it.

IDENTIFYING HIDDEN FILES AND LETTING OLD ANGER GO

Most of us have old memories for which changing the file charges will not be fully effective the first time we try. We will have some files that we are not even able to locate because they are so well hidden. Be patient with yourself. Know this and keep working.

There is a reason any time anything or anyone upsets you or makes you angry. If you can't identify the reason, there probably is a hidden file somewhere. When you have worked the process for dealing with anger and you still haven't found the answers, encourage yourself to look deeper.

In order to get rid of old anger, we need to know what it is about. Once we have pinpointed its origin, we have to ask ourselves, "Why can't I forgive those associated with an old anger? Why can't I forget old anger? Why do I want to hold onto this anger? How is this old anger affecting my life? Would I be happier if I didn't have it? Am I ready to let it go?"

Once you're ready to let old anger go, how do you go about it? Most of us are able to let go of at least some of our angers if we make the commitment to do so and use the process we've talked about throughout this book. Underlined below are some of the key guidelines for those who are grappling with old angers.

Sometimes letting go of old anger is as easy as: recognize what the anger is and what it does to you and then just release it and move on. You may be able to see in a moment that it doesn't fit your present belief system; and that recognition may be enough.

At other times, the anger is in there so deep and you are holding on so tight that you will have great difficulty letting go of it. The anger may agree with your present belief system. If so, you will have to change your beliefs in order to remove the negative charge that you have attached to the memories.

When you consider an old anger, go back and check the content and nature of your perceptions. Practice looking deeply into your perceptions. Resolve to first make peace with yourself and then to make peace with others.

Deal with the feeling underneath the anger. Notice the feeling. Identify the feeling. Claim the feeling. Express the feeling. Just talking out how angry you are or pinpointing the cause of your anger won't rid you of it. In fact, reciting past angers causes you to become angrily aroused again. You buy into your own story of what caused you to have such powerful anger.

In order to let go of old anger, we must forgive. Our unforgiving thoughts are the cause of our suffering. We can be free of suffering by letting go of the past. Go back and review the chapter on forgiveness if you still have forgiveness issues that are holding you back. Remember there is not one thing in this world that should not and could not be forgiven. That is not just some ideal that we can't possibly live up to. It is what is taught by all of the religions of the world. Why do we have so much difficulty accepting the concept? Because we haven't forgiven. Remember, Jesus Christ said, "Father, forgive them for they know not what they do." Remember that there are no old angers or resentments that we can justify holding onto.

Forgiveness is not only a matter of right and wrong—it is a matter of improving your life. You feel better physically when you forgive. Your quality of life improves. Your potential for the future increases. Learn to walk in the other person's shoes, have empathy. Realize that they did the best they could with what they knew and believed at the time.

If you keep running your old angers through the process you've learned in this book and you still can't let go of them, consider getting some help, such as counseling and support groups. You may want to look for help in more than one place. We all respond differently to the various methods that can help us get rid of the anger in our lives. Consider all that is available in order to find what is best for you.

▲

EXERCISE
Forgiveness List

- List all the people you want to forgive, and state what you want to forgive them for.

- After you have made the list, forgive them individually and as a group.

EXERCISE
Taking Inventory of Your "Family Baggage"

Think about your life. Think about what you learned from your family. Using two pieces of paper, write down on one all the stuff you got from your family that has helped you in life, including the values that you still want to hold onto. On the other paper write down the things you got from your family that make you angry or are no longer useful in your life. Think about each item individually; try to think about how it came about, and why you held onto it.

Be grateful for what you got from your parents that was useful. Return to your parents what you no longer want in your life by saying, "Thank you very much, but I don't need this anymore." They never meant to pass their hang-ups onto you in the first place.

Alternative: It may be helpful to have a friend stand in for your parents. It may impact you more if you relate your feelings to another person. In some cases, you may even be able to do this personally, with your parent. You have to consider the effect on them in making this choice.

EXERCISE
Letter of Forgiveness

Write a letter to the person that you want to forgive. Tell them in what way they hurt you. Tell them that you no longer feel the anger and that you have forgiven them. Tell them that you are moving on with your life and that this old anger is no longer a part of it. Send them your love and best wishes for their future. Use your own judgment about whether or not to send this letter to them. If the letter's main impact is reconciliation, you may want to send the letter. On the other hand, if you think it will cause more hurt, do not send it. This letter should not be used in any way to get even.

EXERCISE
Mending Parental Relationships

This is an exercise in which you use visual imagery to deal with the past relationship with your family of origin.

The purpose is to look not only at your upbringing and to forgive all those things that disturb you, but also to remember and appreciate all the things that you learned from your family that have been helpful in your life.

Take out two sheets of paper. On one sheet, make a list of all the things that your family did for you or taught you, gifts that you appreciate and want to keep in your life. Make one list for your mother and one list for your father. Remember that they have nurtured you well enough for you to grow into an independent adult.

On the second sheet of paper, make a list of all those things your family did to you or taught you that you don't want to keep in your life. List the things that disturb you, make your life difficult, or make you angry with your parent. Make a list for each parent. Some things may be listed under both parents.

Now visualize in your mind going into the forest and finding a nice rock alongside of a stream. Sit there for a while and enjoy the beautiful day. When you are ready, visualize taking out your list of the things you got from your parents that you want to keep. Look at each item; remember how you got it. Thank your parents for teaching you this lesson. Appreciate all that they have done for you. If you need to, open your eyes to refresh your memory so you can remember each item on your lists.

Now walk up the stream to where you find a beautiful waterfall. There is a ledge where you can walk under the waterfall. Walk under the waterfall. Let the water cascade gently down on you. Realize how wonderful it feels. Feel it over your whole body.

Now in your mind, take out your lists of items that your parents have given you that you no longer want to keep. Focus on each item individually. Let the water wash it away from you and cleanse you of this old hurt. Take the time to wash away each item on your list. Keep cleansing until each one is completely removed. Do this until every item is completely gone from your body and mind. Rejoice in the awareness that you are now totally free of those old hurts, and you have completely forgiven your parents for each and every hurt.

Be thankful that your parents have given you the good things in your life. They have given you the power to reject the things that are painful to you. Love your parents. Wish them all the best wherever they may be. Appreciate them for what they have given you. Walk away into a new fresh spring day. You see the world more clearly and are ready to embrace it fully, to appreciate the wonders it has to offer. As you walk away with a light heart, you see standing before you, in the path, your parents. You can see that they are delighted to see you. You are surprised and overjoyed to see them. You run toward them. You embrace and love them both. They return the embrace and give their love to you. You are all so excited and happy to meet here at this time. You all walk away together. One of them is holding each of your hands.

Now it is time for them to go back to where they came from. You bid them a joyous goodbye and come back to your present life. You have forgiven your parents for any hurts they have ever given you. You are free from those hurts. They will no longer affect your life. Now come back to the present and enjoy the loving friends that are with you now.

EXERCISE
Shower

Another way to use the above exercise is to actually stand under your shower instead of visualizing a waterfall. This will allow you to incorporate the actual feel of the water and is something you can do on a regular basis whenever you take a shower

---

TOOL
Replacing Old Anger

Any time you feel an old anger affecting you, try to find the source and forgive whoever caused you to feel that way. Next review the event and decide how you would have preferred to respond. Realize that you have now made a new choice in your life. Practice this new behavior in your mind. Rehearse it, and be ready to use it the next time the same or a similar situation arises. If your answer is not satisfactory to you, forgive yourself and try again.

AFFIRMATION

"Today I forgive my parents and release the past."
Repeat this affirmation twenty-five times each day.

Note: You can make up and use an affirmation for any problem that you have difficulty releasing.

Alternative: Write the affirmation down and put it in place you see each day, such as your mirror, refrigerator, desk, or computer.

▼

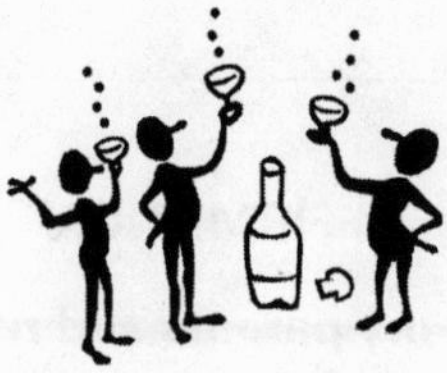

CHAPTER 31

A Life Without Anger!

Ever wonder what it is like to get up every morning and have nothing to be upset about?

Children are able to outgrow all of their temper tantrums when they learn that they are not effective and when they are taught a more effective way to respond. Similarly, as adults we can learn to outgrow all of our anger responses.

Our unforgiving thoughts are the source of our suffering, but we can be free of suffering by letting go of the past. If we want to live in harmony, then we must be in harmony. Love is harmony. Anger is not.

Whatever your age, the present can become the springtime of your life if you allow yourself a rebirth into a new way of feeling and thinking. By living without anger, you can learn to fully enjoy life. Choose to set off on this new path and enjoy the beauty that is present everywhere.

YOU ARE CAPABLE OF CREATING A LIFE WITHOUT ANGER!

To the extent that we are being subconsciously influenced by the past, we are not fully present in any relationship. To the extent that we have resolved past issues, we are capable of thinking, acting, and feeling completely within the present moment. This is when we are the most effective and most likely to act in ways consistent with our thoughts and our feelings.

Most of the time, we think about one thing and do something else. We are most likely to make mistakes when we operate in this way. It is to our advantage to take conscious control of our thoughts, actions, and feelings.

We largely bring on our own emotional disturbances by choosing, both consciously and unconsciously, to think irrationally, to create unhealthy negative feelings, and to act in self-defeating ways. Fortunately, if we know how, we can choose to change our thoughts, feelings, and behaviors.

The first step to change is to build your will power to change your thoughts and your actions. Be determined. Get the knowledge to back your determination. Use your knowledge. Act upon your determination. Follow the methods you have learned. Keep practicing them. They work! The exercises and tools in this book have been put there for your use. You can use the exercises to help you better understand yourself and to help implement any changes you want to make. The tools are there to give you specific techniques that you can use in your daily life to help you remove or deal with any anger. Try them and see how they work for you. Continue to work with the ones that resonate with you. They will be helpful not only in learning not to experience anger, but also in removing or releasing your anger.

Be fully aware of the possibility of changing. Choose a goal, decide to do it, carry it out. Push yourself to implement it. Stick with it until the change is complete.

Having read this book, you have, in effect, been to "Anti-anger School." Now you know that it is not necessary to experience anger. Now you know that you can change the way you feel about things. Whether you use the lessons to change your life to a joyful one is up to you. Consider staying in school until you *graduate* from experiencing anger.

Realize that your old habits die hard, and that anger is a complex problem. But the longer you work to overcome it, the more successful you will become. You may find that it is helpful to re-read this book. Learn and use the tools. Work with the exercises to achieve a meaningful change. You can totally change your life to one of peace and joy. Or you can do nothing to change your old habits—and stay stuck in a life of anger. The choice is yours. The key to change is to make the first commitment. Then learn the steps to achieving change and practice until you reach your goal.

I have enjoyed writing this book because this is the subject closest to my heart. The information I have shared with you transformed my life, and I trust it will also be helpful in changing yours. My sincerest hope is that this book will help you to move beyond anger—and to express more joy in your life.

▲

EXERCISE
Cleansing

Think of an old or new emotional wound that causes you to feel anger. Hold that wound in your mind and think of the word "love." Think of love as cleansing the wound. When we cleanse a wound, it heals itself.

EXERCISE
Breath of Love

Breathe the word love in and out. Breathing is a direct connection with love. With your breath of love, cleanse each angry memory as it arises.

EXERCISE
Experience Nature

Go to your favorite quiet place in nature. Sit quietly at that spot and experience the joy and peace that come over you. Remind yourself that this is our natural state and that the static and negative feelings that we have arise from dealing with other people and events, and that you do not choose to accept these negative feelings in your life any more.

AFFIRMATION

"I release the past. I deserve the best and I am experiencing it."

AFFIRMATION

"I no longer experience anger in my life."

SYMPTOMS OF INNER PEACE

Be on the alert for symptoms of inner peace. The hearts of many people have already been exposed to inner peace. It is possible that others could develop this condition in epidemic proportions. This would pose a serious threat to what has been a relatively stable condition of conflict in the world.

Inner Peace will Enable You to Experience:

- A tendency to think and act spontaneously rather than in response to fears based on past experiences.

- An unmistakable ability to enjoy each moment.

- A loss of interest in judging other people.

- A loss of interest in interpreting the actions of others.

- A loss of interest in conflict.

- A loss of the ability to worry.

- Frequent, overwhelming episodes of appreciation.

- Feelings of contentment with others and nature.

- Frequent attacks of smiling.

- An increasing tendency to let things happen rather than trying to make them happen.

- An increased susceptibility to the love extended by others, as well as the uncontrollable urge to extend it.

WARNING: If you have some, or all of the these symptoms, please be advised that your condition of inner peace may be so far advanced as to be incurable. If you are exposed to anyone exhibiting any of these symptoms, remain exposed only at your own risk!

Workshops, Seminars and Lectures

Given by **Dean Van Leuven**

Dean Van Leuven is an international speaker and regularly conducts seminars, lectures and workshops in learning to live without anger and related quality of life issues. This book is based on the materials that he presents at those events.

For an up-to-date schedule of Dean's Life Without Anger events, refer to his web site www.lifewithoutanger.com. To contact him for an event in your area, e-mail him at drdean@lifewithoutanger.com; or call 1-800-359-6015.

Seminars and Lectures
These are usually about 2 to 3 hours in length and are designed as an introduction to the concept of learning to live without anger.

Weekend Workshops
The weekend workshops involve learning and working with the basic concepts of learning to live without anger. Participants learn to develop an individualized plan for removing anger from their life. It is helpful for those attending these workshops to have read the book in advance.

Parenting or Partnering Workshops and Seminars

These workshops and seminars involve learning new skills to use in your daily lives to raise your children anger free or to enrich the relationship with your partner by ridding yourselves of anger.

Custom Designed Workshops and Seminars

Normally designed for business or professional organizations, in these gatherings participants learn to use the concept of living without anger as it applies to the needs and operation of their business or service organization.

Instructor Training

This program teaches participants how to present the Life Without Anger material to others.

If you are interested in attending any of these sessions or arranging for a specific program for your group, please contact us and we will make every effort to accommodate you.

Thank You!

for selecting this book from DeVorss Publications. If you would like
to receive a complete catalog of our specialized selection of current
and classic Metaphysical, Spiritual, Inspirational, Self-Help, and New
Thought books, please visit our website or give us a call and ask for
your free copy.

DeVorss Publications
devorss.com • 800-843-5743